BLACKS, WHITES AND BLUES

series edited by Paul Oliver

BLACKS WHITES AND BLUES

Tony Russell

STEIN AND DAY / *Publishers* / New York

First published, in both hard cover and paperback editions, in the United States of America by Stein and Day / *Publishers* / 1970.

Printed in England
Stein and Day / *Publishers* / 7 East 48 Street, New York, N.Y. 10017
SBN 8128-1316-2 (hard cover)
    8128-1320-0 (paperback)

Produced by November Books Limited
Designed by Ian Cameron
House editor: Elizabeth Kingsley-Rowe

The illustrative material for this book has been taken largely from record companies' catalogues and publicity documents of the period, and from record labels reproduced from the originals. For the loan of much of this material the author is grateful to Paul Oliver, Robert M. W. Dixon, Bob Yates, Bruce Bastin, Chris Comber and George W. Tye.

Contents

FOREWORD   6

MINSTRELSY   8

OLD FAMILIAR TUNES   25

LETTING OUT THE BLUES   48

'THAT'S THE IDEA OF
        THE WHITE PEOPLE'   59

OUT WEST   78

OUT EAST   93

BIBLIOGRAPHY   103

DISCOGRAPHY   105

INDEX   110

Foreword

This book attempts to draw together two lines of discussion that have up to now been almost completely separate. There are numerous books and articles on Afro-American folk music, and some on white American folk music, but this is the first essay which looks at both traditions and tries to describe their interaction. I hope it will be, if nothing else, a stimulus to new arguments and research topics, and a lead to new listening experiences.

With that aim in mind, I have referred often to recordings which the reader can find without much difficulty: to LPs rather than the original 78s. The code numbers in the text refer either to albums by individual artists or groups (in the form 01.1 and so forth), or to anthologies (which appear as A1 onwards). If a cited recording has no code, either it has not been reissued or it is available on a reissue which contains few or no other items of relevance to our subject. The LPs and EPs to which the codes refer are listed in the Discography; at the time of writing most of them are still in catalogue. If I had had twice as many pages, I should have provided footnotes, original catalogue numbers, page-references and all the rest of it; but I had not, so I must leave the enquiring reader with a good deal of further research on his plate. However, as I found when doing it myself, it is research that repays the labour well.

I have not been stringent with terminology. White traditions are described indiscriminately as 'country', 'hillbilly' and 'old time'; 'blues' sometimes stands for 'black blues' and sometimes does not. I have not always stated the colour of a musician; in such cases it should be obvious from the context. Nor is there much biography, but gaps can be filled by consulting the standard works listed in the Bibliography. I have assumed an acquaintance with American folk music in my reader, but I have certainly not written for expert collectors or ethnomusicologists.

The evidence for musical exchange is enormous, and starts piling up as far back as the 1820s. I could not cover a century and a half in this book, so I brought my account to a ragged halt in the late 1930s. The subsequent thirty-odd years will be the subject of a second volume.

In writing this essay I plundered the published and unpublished work of many researchers, to whom I apologise – for space prevented me from acknowledging them very often in the text – and give hearty thanks. Information on black matters came from Bruce Bastin, John Houlston Cowley, Bob Dixon, David Evans, John Godrich, Bob Groom of *Blues World*, Karl Gert zur Heide, Don Kent, and Mike Leadbitter and Simon Napier of *Blues Unlimited*; on white, from Joe E. Bussard, Jr, John Cohen, Norm Cohen of the John Edwards Memorial Foundation, Dave Freeman of County Records, Archie Green, John B. Larsen and Bill C. Malone. Albert McCarthy of *Jazz Monthly* lent magazines, George Tye photographs, Bert Whyatt recording-files; Dave Crosbie, David Pritchard, Francis Smith, Jim Vyse and David West assembled invaluable tapes. I owe much to Chris Comber, who supplied photographs, tapes and information without stint, and introduced me to some great music. Much, too, to my friend and fellow enthusiast Bob Yates, who gave me access to many a quaint and curious volume of forgotten lore.

To the Series Editor, Paul Oliver, I owe a tremendous debt. Not content with giving me the opportunity to write this book, he provided records, photographic material, information and encouragement. For all these, but especially for the constant and friendly encouragement, my deepest thanks.

I built this book on a conviction: that, whether or not my own views had anything to them, the musicians I was talking about had something worthwhile to say. Yet many of them, including some of the greatest artists, are almost forgotten. I shall be very happy if *Blacks, Whites & Blues* helps to give them the recognition they deserve.

Minstrelsy

'It's not very much of song that Negro got from white, because Negro people always was a kind of a singing group of people. You see, we was kind of a little different; we were a segregated bunch from down among the white people. The white man could get education and he could learn proper things like read a note, and the Negro couldn't. All he had to get from his music what God give him in his heart. And that's the only thing he got. And he didn't get that from the white man; God give it to him.'

The speaker was Willie Thomas, factory janitor and guitarist of Scotlandville, La., talking to Paul Oliver in 1960 (A11). He is a preacher, which explains his notion of the divine inspiration of black song; surprisingly, he is also a blues singer. (Surprisingly, because to the religious man blues are devil music; 'A man who's singing the blues,' said Lil' Son Jackson in retirement, 'I think it's a sin because it cause other people to sin.' But Thomas takes a broad and kindly view: 'It ain't nothin' to do with bein' against God . . . if it comes nach'al, *church* people sing the blues.') It is not evident from his remarks that Thomas was equating black song with the blues; but he was born in 1912, and by the time he was listening at all closely to music the blues had risen to great heights of popularity. The first generation of blues singers was born twenty or thirty years earlier.

What he did not say was whether whites got very much of song from black people. There were many thousands of poor whites who couldn't get education, nor learn to read a note; and most rural communities could fairly claim to have been 'singing groups of people' for as long as anyone could remember. It would be possible to make a case for an equally independent tradition of white song. In fact, neither tradition developed independently of the other; the races lived too close together, and each relied upon the other's support too much for any real cultural separation. 'Negro entered into White man,' wrote W. J. Cash, 'as profoundly as White man entered into Negro – subtly influencing every gesture, every word, every emotion and idea, every attitude.' Though the blacks were 'a segregated bunch', they received and passed out countless musical ideas from surrounding peoples –

Photograph: Butch Cage (fiddle) and Willie Thomas, Zachary, La.

not merely southern, Anglo-Saxon whites, but French-speaking cajuns, Mexicans, and perhaps even the German-, Italian- and Swedish-speaking immigrants.' Their influence upon the folk music of other ethnic groups has perhaps been greater than the sum of influences from those peoples upon themselves, but in this book I hope to look at a few examples of both black-on-white and white-on-black impressions. The black man's contribution to the body of world folk music is nowadays widely recognised, but too often it is thought to stop at the blues, jazz and spirituals: the black people's most personal creations. It is nearly as important to see that white country music in America would not have its present form if it were not for black workmanship. Indeed, the only way to understand fully the various folk musics of America is to see them as units in a whole; as traditions with, to be sure, a certain degree of independence, but possessing an overall unity.

Consider the landscape. A musician would be open to sounds from every direction: from family and friends, from field and railroad yard, lumber camp and mine; from street singers and travelling show musicians; from phonograph records and radio; from dances and suppers and camp-meetings and carnivals; from fellow prisoners in jails, from fellow workmen everywhere. A white youngster could learn a song or a tune not only in the bosom of his family but from their black employees – mammy, Uncle Remus or anyone else. Racial antipathy, of course, hampered the free exchange of musical ideas, and it will become clear, in this book, that interaction was more fertile in areas where blacks were scattered and thus less fearful. Nevertheless, in all but the most tightly enclosed communities, there was some degree of interaction, and, as the twentieth century grew older, and group isolation rarer, the threads of the two traditions were more and more often entangled. Moreover, there were always musicians to whom musical values were more important than racist ones, men who would not care a jot if they, as whites, happened to like black pieces, or vice versa. Again, there were certain forms of musical expression to which it seems absurd to attach any racial origin or ownership; who, for instance, can say whether harmonica solos imitating trains or hunting scenes were first played by blacks or by whites? And lastly, while it is possible to pick out strains that are peculiarly black or peculiarly white, what can we say about the music of those who were neither? What 'ought' to be the song of the mulatto?

The answer to most of the questions about song origins is

simply that there can be no answer. We can only trace country music back into the latter part of the nineteenth century, and as far as that only with difficulty; blues are an enigma until the 'teens of the present century. We can begin the story only where our information begins; and we cannot ever be sure that we are not misrepresenting history. Recordings, which are much used in this book, can tell a deceptive tale; interviews are hard to get and often hard to believe. A folk tradition has no starting point, and most folk songs are like most jokes; everybody knows them, but nobody knows who invented them.

Nevertheless, we can go back several generations and find something about the work of the blacks and whites as a 'singing group of people'. We can go into the churches for hymns, into the mountain villages and little-visited flatlands for Celtic ballads; but let us go rather into the theatres of the cities, for the minstrel song. Let us consider vaudeville's grandfather.

'In the eighteen-forties,' wrote Newman Ivey White, 'Negro music, for the first time, spread beyond the plantation.' Through songs like *Zip Coon* and *Jim Crow* a vogue for slave music was created which took the entertainment world by storm. A gentleman writing in *Putnam's Monthly* in 1855, and speaking as a slave-owning planter, pronounced the 'coon' songs truly representative of black music-making. Not that, on stage, they were to be heard much from blacks; the minstrelsy of the plantation was presented by white actors in blackface. Among the most famous bands of minstrels were the Christy and Moore & Burgess troupes, both of which toured extensively in America and Europe. The performers wore evening dress, and, in the words of a Christy advertisement of about 1871, 'anything appertaining to vulgarity' was 'strictly excluded'. 'Fun', Moore & Burgess chimed in, 'Without Vulgarity'. In a Moore & Burgess songbook of the period can be seen attempts to give authenticity to the whole minstrel genre; 'undoubtedly many of the negro melodies we hear today were, roughly, songs as were sung by the slaves hundreds of years ago – music that was never put upon paper, but handed down from one band to another.' There is much virtue in that 'roughly'. This was an age, remember, when folksongs were relentlessly 'improved', even by quite reputable field collectors. The author goes on to tell a story about Eugene Stratton, the white Alsatian-American 'Whistling Coon'. Questioned about a 'peculiar and exceeding pretty song' in his repertoire, Stratton explained, 'You see that young man over there? . . . He was a

POOR OLD JOE,

Song & Chorus,

SUNG BY THE

Christy Minstrels,

COMPOSED BY

S. C. FOSTER.

slave, and the song you have just heard was one they used to sing upon their plantation. He hummed it over to me and I have set it to music. But it's a very difficult thing to set coon songs to music.' To ease the difficulty Stratton employed compositions by professional writers like Leslie Stuart, who provided him with *Little Dolly Daydream* and the immortal *Lily Of Laguna*, a 'coon' love-ditty expressed in words very far removed from plantation speech. Of course, songs like these have no folk status – though *Laguna*, as a public-house 'standard', is taking on some of the characteristics of a folk song – but they have been popular, at times, with the folk; and the minstrel show did not die in its home country, but went out on the road, bringing to the rural audiences some of the sentimental coonery and a lot of corny comic routines. (Minstrels in the south probably observed less strict canons of taste than did the original dinner-jacketed ones.)

After the blackface shows came the music-hall. It is difficult to determine which characteristics of music-hall were purely American and which English (and which shared), but each country sent popular ideas to the other, and, if Stratton and his disciple G. H.

Elliott, 'The Chocolate-Coloured Coon', made one kind of Americana appealing in England, there was certainly an enthusiastic response in the States to such gems of the music-hall era as *Champagne Charlie Is My Name*, *If You Were The Only Girl In The World* and *She Was Poor But She Was Honest*. America's own contributions were numerous and in many cases enduring; Paul Dresser's *The Letter That Never Came* (1886), Harry von Tilzer's *Good-Bye, Eliza Jane* (1903) and *A Bird In A Gilded Cage* (1900), and Charles K. Harris's *There'll Come A Time* (1895) were all recorded several times by rural singers and issued in the 'hillbilly series' of the major recording companies. Other favourites that moved from stage or drawing-room to country shack were *The Fatal Wedding* (1893) and *In The Baggage Coach Ahead* (1896), a pair of tragic songs written by Gussie L. Davis and thereafter much recorded. Ernest V. Stoneman and Charlie Poole's North Carolina Ramblers, for instance, between them recorded versions of five of the last six titles. Unlike some of the artists whose records appeared in the hillbilly listings, Stoneman and Poole were authentic countrymen, and so they sounded; but these

Below: Charlie Poole (banjo), Posey Rorer (fiddle), Roy Harvey (guitar): the North Carolina Ramblers.

music-hall songs had a place in their repertoire just as much as the ballads and dance-tunes. The interesting thing about Davis's compositions is that they were the work of a black man. Davis once swept the halls of the Cincinnati Conservatory of Music – 'incidentally picking up some of the elements of composition', as Spaeth remarks – and at another time was a railroad porter, which experience inspired *Baggage Coach*. He provides a copiously documentable example of a black figure passing material into white tradition (mainly white, for very few blacks sang his ballads), but of course this is all some way beyond folk areas – at this point in tradition, at least – and it is clear from the songs themselves that Davis, like the many other black vaudevillians, was working in a style basically white in the first place. However, the acceptance of his compositions, and others like them by both black and white musicians, was so considerable in the country communities that a mention of these vaudeville days is essential in any study of early twentieth century folksong. Rural musicians were very frequently no more than frustrated vaudevillians; and the urban parlour ballads or musical stage hits were by no means always thought too classy for reproduction in country society. For instance, there is a 'twenties poster advertising a visit by the Carolina Tar Heels (Doc. Walsh and Garley Foster), which, though offering 'Honest-To-Goodness String Music Of The Hills', does inform

A third Tar Heel was Clarence 'Tom' Ashley, who died in 1967.

CAROLINA TAR HEELS

VICTOR AND COLUMBIA RECORDING ARTISTS
— RADIO ARTISTS —

DOC. WALSH
The Banjo King of The Carolinas
— WITH —

GARLEY FOSTER
The Human Bird

ARTISTS IN THE RENDITION OF POPULAR NUMBERS THAT TOUCH THE HEART, MAKE YOU LAUGH OR PUT A TICKLE IN YOUR FEET

GARLEY FOSTER

DOC. WALSH

GID

TANNER

Left: 'Mac and Bob', who met at the Kentucky Blind School. Right: James Gideon Tanner, 1885–1960.

the passer-by that Doc. will 'entertain (him) with . . . old time Southern Songs mingled with the latest Broadway Hits'. This 'unusual program of high class entertainment' was no doubt being duplicated all over the countryside. For example, by the Carter Family, whose advertisements claimed 'This Program Is Morally Good'. By McFarland and Gardner, 'The Brunswick Recording Artist (sic) . . . hear them in person, old songs, new songs and any thing you like to hear, on most any instrument . . . A good Time for young and old.' By the 'Rip Roarin', Snortin', Burn 'Em Up String Band', Gid Tanner's Georgia Skillet-Lickers. Tanner's men used to perform *It's A Long Way To Tipperary* and *The Dark Town Strutters' Ball*, which, published in 1912 and 1915 respectively, would scarcely have been the *latest* Broadway hits, but personal appearances by the group would no doubt have featured solo spots by their blind guitarist Riley Puckett, whose immense repertoire included many popular songs of the 'twenties, some of which were issued not very long after the 'straight' dance bands' and crooners' renditions as, so to speak, countrymen's versions.

The black debt to stage music, however, took a different form. One of Riley Puckett's recordings was *On The Other Side Of Jordan* (36.1), also put on disc by Uncle Dave Macon (31.1). The tune, and possibly the words, of this merry piece were by Dan Emmett, and were published in 1853 as *Jordan Am A Hard Road To Travel*. The 'am' betrays the origin: it was a 'nigger minstrel' piece, and not surprisingly, for Emmett was the doyen of minstreldom, strengthening the foundations laid by Thomas 'Daddy' Rice (composer of *Jim Crow*) and laying a way for the Christys and the other troupes. While *Jordan* did not survive, in black circles, into the recording era, there were minstrel tunes that lived on; *Zip Coon* became *Turkey In The Straw*, while the jig *Buffalo Gals* was recorded under that name and as *Round Town Gals* or *Alabama Gal, Won't You Come Out Tonight?* It was possible to hear it in Nashville only a few years ago, played by Blind James Campbell and his street band (07.1). Chris Strachwitz, who recorded this black group for his Arhoolie label, commented in his notes, 'on this record the blues dominate since the group knew that my interests were mainly in that direction. Their work on the street and at social functions includes many more sentimental and pop numbers . . .' Campbell and his fiddle player Beauford Clay were both born in the first decade of this century, so could well have known those latter-day minstrel pieces which seem to have been popular among blacks and whites then; pieces like *I Got Mine* and *Chicken, You Can't Roost Too High For Me*, also known as *Chicken, You Can Roost Behind The Moon*, under which title it was recorded by the black Memphis singer Frank Stokes in 1927 (40.1). *I Got Mine* was much collected by White's informants (from blacks), and he refers to it, writing in 1928, as a 'popular vaudeville song about twenty years ago'; records are very numerous, and among them is a version (A3) by, again, Frank Stokes, who also performed *You Shall (Be Free)* (40.1), a sardonic song very extensively popular among blacks in these years and found all over the place in White's and Scarborough's collections. *Chicken* is probably the piece published in 1899 under the names of Cole, Johnson and Accooe, and it is thus distinctive in that the composers were black; Bob Cole and J. Rosamond Johnson were perhaps the best known of all black vaudeville writers and singers in the turn-of-the-century years. (J. Rosamond's brother, James Weldon Johnson, who worked with the team, became a distinguished poet and secretary of the NAACP.) *Chicken* embodied the belief that all blacks were chicken stealers, and it is a little strange that Stokes, Pink Anderson (01.3) and other black artists were willing to propagate it, or the similar sentiments of *I Got Mine*, which tells the story of a man who 'went down to a little crap

16

Riley Puckett, the most versatile and prolific of the early recording stars. He died in 1946.

game' and lost every penny that he had in his pocket, except for that folk-singer's standby, a greenback dollar bill. The police raid the joint, and in the furore the singer 'gets his', so ever since he's 'been livin'' high on chicken and wine', a 'member of the knock-down society'. Of course this sort of thing would go down well at white dances, and it is not surprising that whites, like the talking bluesman Chris Bouchillon of South Carolina, found it appealing;

CHRIS BOUCHILLON

"The Talking Comedian of the South"

WHEN Chris Bouchillon says anything he does it in such a dry, humorous sort of way that you can't help but laugh.

Chris isn't averse to a bit of playing and singing, now and then, either. When he tunes up his voice and guitar, folks come from miles around to hear the melodies of this popular South Carolina minstrel.

In addition to being one of the foremost wits and singers of the South, Chris can tinker with an auto just as effectively as with a tune.

CHRIS BOUCHILLON

and the popular chorus of *You Shall Be Free*,

> Oh, well, you see that preacher laid behind the log,
>   A hand on the trigger, got his eye on the hog;
> The hog said 'Hmm!', the gun said 'Biff!';
>   Jumped on the hog with all the dripping . . .

was taken up by the Georgian fiddler Earl Johnson (A18) and the Virginian guitarist Frank Hutchison, and by many black singers as an element of the common anti-clerical theme. On race records the anti-black sentiments of these early songs are generally redirected against sections of the black public – preachers, wife-stealers, fast life women, and so forth – whereas the originals obviously poked fun, sometimes goodnatured and sometimes not, at black people in general. As White remarks, 'the Negro minstrel song, like many of the novels of ante-bellum southern life, was commonly used as an instrument of propaganda against the interests of the Negro himself.' This is obviously true, so, faced with the records of blacks singing 'coon' songs, one may choose to believe either that the singers were Uncle Tomming, or that they were mocking the originals. The latter is, I think, closer to the truth. With what intent white singers used the material it is diffi-

18

cult to say, unless one knows the individual singer's views on colour, but, granted that some hillbilly artists would have shrunk from the faintest suspicion of nigger-loving, it is probable that their coon songs preserved, and indeed intensified, the racist flavour which they initially possessed.

Coon songs were not always comic; there were also the sentimental 'darky' effusions, the great line that stretched each side of *Old Black Joe.* Judging black life by these – as European audiences very probably did in watching the 'nigger minstrel' shows, having nothing else to go on – one summons up a peaceful picture of woolly-headed slaves strumming their banjos, fishing in the sun and courting little octoroons with improbable names. When they were young they used to wait, on massa's table lay de

'Darky ditties' from a Victor catalogue of c. *1903. Bert Williams is the only black, rather than black-face, artist.*

COMIC AND COON SONGS

By ARTHUR COLLINS

V 409 Cindy, I Dreams About You
  1635 Down Where the Wurzburger Flows
V 538 Every Race Has a Flag But the Coon
  2408 Every Morn I Bring Her Chicken
    A Burlesque on "Violets"
  1632 Helen Gonne
V 157 I Ain't Seen No Messenger Boy
  1629 I Just Can't Help From Loving That Man
  1965 I Wonder Why Bill Bailey Don't
    Come Home
  160 I'd Leave My Happy Home for You
  1631 If Money Talks, It Aint on Speakin'
    Terms With Me
  647 If You Love Your Baby, Make
    Goo Goo Eyes
  2051 I'll Be Busy All Next Week A colored lady's
    excuses to an unwelcome suitor
  2052 I'm a Jonah Man Bert Williams' tremendous
    hit with Williams & Walker
  2411 I'm Thinkin' of You All o'de While
  650 I've Got a White Man Workin' for Me
  651 Just Because She Made dem Goo Goo Eyes
V 163 Mandy Lee   Chattaway
  1634 My Maid From Hindostan
  162 Old Bill Jones Rube Song

  2153 Oh! My! A Harrowing Tale of a Colored Belle
    a Pig and an Apple Dumpling
  1630 Please Let Me Sleep Wail of a Weary Coon
  158 Pliny, Come Kiss Your Baby
V 539 Strike Up the Band
  1964 The Pooh Bah of Blackville Town
  2425 The Gambling Man
  1633 Under the Bamboo Tree   Cole
V 170 Vaudeville Specialty
  2407 You Can't Fool All de People All de Time

By BERT. A WILLIAMS

  994 All Going Out and Nothing Coming In
  991 My Castle on the Nile
  993 Where Was Moses when the Light
    Went Out

VICTOR, Seven-Inch, 50c. Each, $5.00 Per Dozen
MONARCH, Ten-Inch, $1.00 Each, $10.00 Per Dozen

COON SONGS WITH BANJO

By SPENCER and OSSMAN

  617 Coon, Coon, Coon
  820 Hot Times on the Levee
  1711 My Girl from Dixie
  1710 On Emancipation Day
  818 That Minstrel Man of Mine
  816 The Colored Major
  819 The Little Old Log Cabin in the Lane

ORIGINAL NEGRO SONGS AND SHOUTS

By BILLY GOLDEN

  68 Bye Bye, Ma Honey
  617 Crap Shooting
  622 Rabbit Hash Just Coon Nonsense
  616 Roll on de Ground
V 618 The Mocking Bird Whistling Solo
  619 The Wedding O'er the Hill
  65 Turkey in de Straw
  621 Uncle Jefferson
  620 Yaller Gal Laughing Song

By GEORGE W. JOHNSON, the Whistling Coon

  584 The Laughing Coon
  583 The Laughing Song
  582 The Whistling Coon
  581 The Whistling Girl

DUETS

By DUDLEY and MACDONOUGH

  1329 Bye and Bye You Will Forget Me
  1076 In the Shadow of the Pines

plate, and so on, but in these songs they are generally old and venerable. They raise their voices in lamentation when *Massa's In De Cold Cold Ground*, but not, one feels sure, in exultation to *Shout, Mourner, You Shall Be Free* – except perhaps in the safe metaphors of a hymn. Of chain-gangs and beatings and slave-drivers we hear not a whisper; nor of massa's hot intentions towards the estate's little octoroons, though that particular abuse was sometimes romanticised into such songs as *My Pretty Quadroon*.

> Massa had gardens and bowers,
>   And flowers that were always in bloom;
> He begrudged me my pretty wild flower,
>   Cora, my pretty quadroon.

And the separation of lovers was commemorated by pieces like *Lorena*, a mid-nineteenth century weepie which was sung, movingly enough in its way, by the Blue Sky Boys (A22) and others. On the 'peculiar institution' itself songs were somewhat taciturn, and Fields Ward's *Those Cruel Slavery Days* (46.1) is exceptional:

> On the day old master died, all the darkies stood
>   and cried,
>   In those agonising cruel slavery days;
> For we knew we must be sold for the silver and the gold,
>   In those agonising cruel slavery days.
>
> Well, they sold my brother Sam to a man from Alabam',
>   My sister went to Georgia far away;
> Then they broke my heart for life when they sold my
>   loving wife,
>   In those agonising cruel slavery days.

The singer goes on to reminisce about 'days of long ago', when 'the darkies all would sing and the banjo it would ring'; and he looks forward to the time when 'there never will be cruel slavery days'. Unless the song is repulsively satirical, it has a liberality rare in southern expression; the language may be minstrel-flavoured, but the verdict on slavery days – 'agonising, cruel' – is unequivocal. For various comprehensible reasons, songs explicitly about slavery were recorded only by whites; blacks may have sung them in private, but no one would have encouraged them to perform them when white men were around. And when whites did make records about blacks they tended rather to be comfortably commercial couplings like the Skillet-Lickers' *Run, Nigger Run* and *Dixie*, which, with its affirmation of the southern values of home pride and nigger-hating, would ensure for the band a warm welcome in any port-of-call.

The Fields Ward song just spoken of was made for Gennett Records, an Indiana firm which put out blues, country music and jazz, along with conventional popular material, in a multitude of series, and also pressed discs for private concerns. Some of these have survived, among them a few with a 'KKK' label, showing a fiery cross in gold on scarlet; the featured group is the '100% Americans', and one title is *Why I Am A Klansman*. The band's name was taken from the Klan periodical *The One Hundred Percent American*; their song, like most Klan pronouncements of

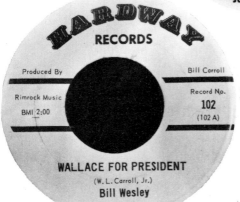

those days, is vague about the organization's aims and nowhere mentions blacks; the keywords are 'God', 'my country' and 'honour'. There is a story that the local Klavern in Birmingham, Ala., for a time managed the black harmonica player Jaybird Coleman, which is odd, for Coleman, on the recorded evidence at least, had no truck with white music. Probably the Klan's interest was purely financial. It was an Alabamian, incidentally, who revived the KKK in the early twentieth century, one Colonel William Joseph Simmons, of whom Randel relates 'his Negro "mammy" had often regaled him with exciting Klan stories'. Stone Mountain, where he rekindled the Klan torch, is an unmissable landmark outside Atlanta. The organization's work in that city throve with the help of country music; Fiddlin' John Carson regularly played for Klan functions. Fifty years later an identical mood can be observed on the 'Reb Rebel' records that issue from a Crowley, La., store. *NAACP Flight 105* is reputed to have sold a million, and may even be heard – it is said – on black jukeboxes; its jokes, for all their racism, are much less offensive than the grotesque sophistries of *Looking For A Handout*, which urges blacks to quit the breadlines and get decent jobs, or the vile *Kajun Klu Klux Klan* (sic). These underground discs use all the resources of country music to back their message; indeed, a rumour is circulating that 'Johnny Rebel' hides one of Nashville's most famous personalities. Students of American politics will also remember that the George Wallace bandwagon has its wheels greased by hillbilly bands; W. Lee 'Pappy' O'Daniel rode to the Texas state governorship on the same mixture of populism, old-time religion and country music.

The relationship between the Klan and Jaybird Coleman may be apocryphal. There are, however, plenty of instances of white interest in black musicians; many of the latter, for example, received their first instrument from white men – like Fred McDowell, who had reason to thank 'Mr Taylor, a white man from Texas'. Then, race records are turned up in white homes, though exactly *what* records, in *what* homes, no one has been concerned to find out. Whether blacks bought hillbilly records to any extent is less certain, but we have a clear account of a broadminded black family from John Jackson of Fairfax, Va. John's sister played the piano, and her mail-ordered discs were mainly classical; his father bought blues records; he himself listened to a variety of material, from Jim Jackson to Jimmie Rodgers, Brownie McGhee to the Delmore Brothers.

Furthermore, there were dozens of hillbilly records on the market before the black singers of the south ever got on disc; a rural black in search of traditional music before about 1926 would have had to be satisfied with white artists. When Bill Helms, the Georgia-born fiddler, first heard the early (*circa* 1924) discs of Gid Tanner and Riley Puckett, it was on a phonograph owned by 'an old darkey out in the country'.

Old Familiar Tunes

It has been said that the advent of phonograph recording in rural areas spelled the death of folk traditions, because the record ironed out regional characteristics and killed off all the forms which did not have widespread popularity. It is true enough that blues played a less dominant role than recordings suggest. But formal and stylistic qualities peculiar to a single region or school could be observed for some years, as one may see from the dozens of reissue collections which have been compiled on purely regional lines. Moreover, much recording activity was directed quite deliberately at regional markets.

The concept of the record as trend-setter is recent; in the 'twenties and 'thirties rural music was generally put on disc in order to meet an already established demand. Certain forms were undeniably ill served; Columbia's talent scout Frank Walker has testified that company policy did not permit much coverage of old ballads, or banjo or autoharp tunes. And mountain dulcimer music appears on a disproportionately tiny number of discs. Black stringbands were poorly documented, too; the Wright family, for instance, who had an importance and repute in Texas at least as great as the Chatmans in Mississippi, never made a record. Perhaps a high-level decision was passed that the neat categories of the 'race' and 'old time' catalogues should be maintained as far as possible; if so, it was only partly successful. The Mississippi Sheiks, that is the Chatmans, appeared more than once in the old time listings, while the white Allen Brothers turned up in the Columbia race series. (For this they sued the company for $250,000, but they lost the case and the record remained where it was.) Then the Carver Brothers, a black group including the young Josh White, were marketed largely through Paramount's hillbilly listing. On the whole, of course, the old time catalogue purveyed white, and the race catalogue black material; but each list suffered musical infiltration from, and occasionally echoed distinctive sounds in, the other. And by the 'thirties the dichotomy had disappeared, black and white country material now being issued in common series. (Decca was the one exception.) The disc labels preserved the pigeon-holes with phrases like 'race blues' or 'old time singing', but not exclusively; many of the Memphis Jug Band's last recordings, for example, were described as 'novelty hot dance'.

During the 'thirties, too, the accusations of 'detraditionalisation' and 'deregionalisation' do become appropriate; but in this, again, the industry was often reflecting migration-patterns and other changes in the social behaviour of the south and ex-southerners. Back in the 'twenties the recorded music of country folk really was representative of most of the stronger traditions. This is a point worth stressing, for there are scholars who would dismiss all this talk of phonograph recordings as matter irrelevant to the study of folk music. To side with these stern guardians is to misunderstand the folk process; the bearers of tradition are not purists, but eclectics. They will devour ditties from records with the same enthusiasm as they imbibe songs learned at mother's knee or other unimpeachably oral sources. Indeed, the whole business of 'oral tradition' is being reshaped by new media; to scorn the record is to ignore one of the most potent diffusers of folk-usable material. There is the radio, too; the shaping role of those old time music hours, and guitar and mandolin clubs, could well be investigated. Had it not been for Fiddlin' John Carson's popularity over WSB, Atlanta, there would have been no impetus behind the OKeh field-trip of June 1923, and the great recording journeys of the decade might never have taken place. No, the enthusiastic response with which the early phonograph discs were greeted, even among the poorest country people, proves that their advertisement as 'old time tunes' was fair. What southerners wanted to hear on record were, as an OKeh catalogue put it, 'melodies (which) will quicken the memory of the tunes of yesterday'; melodies, that is, sung and played in traditional mode by musicians steeped in tradition. There is every reason to believe that that was exactly what they got.

These records do something else; they confirm a suspicion which must come to everyone who reads through the text collections and reminiscences of the early twentieth century. The traditional music of the countryman was a repertoire shared by black and white; a common stock. Some tunes or songs might be associated by some of their users with one race rather than the other, but most would have no racial connotations. This sharing both stemmed from and resulted in an extraordinary variety of musical approaches. Pieces from the common stock could be performed equally comfortably by the solo singer with any kind of instrument or none; by duet, trio or quartet, or a combination of any size; by the brass band, the string band and the jazz band. And this adaptability is itself linked with the function of the music: group entertainment, particularly at dances. The old-time musician of either colour will, as often as not, describe a tune according to the kind of dance it accompanies; waltz or quickstep, slow drag or buck-dance, breakdown, shimmy or grind. (A lot of confusion arises from the fact that a popular dance of the 'twenties, and possibly earlier, was called the Blues. Many blues (songs) are Blues, but not all Blues are blues.) Further, since dance functions have subtle social differences, the music could not become absolutely standardised; what was played, and the manner in which it was played, would depend on the social standing of the guests, their age, their colour, their mood, and their degree of musical appreciation.

What was this common stock? First, there were the ballads of

Photographs: Fiddlin' John Carson (left) – circus barker, moonshiner and medicine showman. His The Old Hen Cackled And The Rooster's Going to Crow *helped to open the country-music market;* Dalhart's Wreck Of The Old 97 *expanded it nation-wide.*

VERNON DALHART

hero or antihero: *Casey Jones*, *John Henry*, *Stack O'Lee*, *Railroad Bill*, *Delia*, *Frankie And Johnny*, *Joe Turner Blues*; one might add *He's In The Jailhouse Now*, *Bully Of The Town*, and, in a sense, *Boll Weevil*. There were songs of gamblers: *Don't Let The Deal Go Down* and *Jack O' Diamonds* (and *Stack O'Lee* again). Of low life generally: *Ain't Nobody's Business* and *Mama Don't Allow*, *Salty Dog* and *Easy Rider*, *Drunken Spree* and *All Night Long;* *Raise A Rucus Tonight*, *Chicken*, *I Got Mine*, even the aged adultery-song *Our Goodman* (known generally as *Three – Four*, *Five*, *Six*, *Seven – Nights Experience*). The powerful appeal of the locomotive, and the associated themes of separation, loneliness and homesickness, are expressed in *Poor Boy*, *Long Way From Home* and *A Hundred Miles* (or *Five Hundred Miles*, or *Old Reuben*); in *Lonesome Road Blues* ('Going down that road feeling bad . . .'), *Red River Blues* and *Look Up, Look Down;* and, evocatively, in the melancholy tune which is best known, perhaps, through the Memphis Jug Band's version, *K. C. Moan* (A16). There is the tender *Corrine Corrina*, with which we may group *Careless Love* and *Make Me A Pallet On The Floor*. Then the pieces with instrumental rather than thematic similarities; the fiddle and the banjo tunes which draw on a huge collection of couplets and quatrains that are nearly all interchangeable from piece to piece. Such are *Sourwood Mountain* and *Old Hen Cackle*, *Bile Dem Cabbage Down*, *Turkey In The Straw*, *Big Ball In Town*, *Leather Britches*, *Buffalo Gals*, and the *Rabbit In The Log/Pay Day/Keep My Skillet Good And Greasy* group. From the jazz-composers came *Wang Wang Blues*, *St Louis Blues* and *Beale Street Blues*, as well as *Hot Time In The Old Town Tonight* and *At The Dark Town Strutters' Ball*. From earlier times: *Redwing*, *Little Brown Jug*, *It Ain't Gonna Rain No More*; *Arkansas Traveler* and *Travelin' Man*; *Old Dan Tucker* and *Old Black Joe*. Equally old were the hymns *Mary Don't You Weep*, *Give Me That Old Time Religion*, *No Hiding Place Down There*, and many others which were firmly common-stock by the turn of the century if not earlier.

One could group these songs and tunes in a dozen ways; they are arranged above only for a sort of conciseness. Some, admittedly, are better covered on records by whites than by blacks, or vice versa, but documentary work by ethnomusicologists, together with musicians' reminiscences, substantially corrects this

Opposite: selected verses show both composed and traditional elements. No. 10 occurs in blues by Ma Rainey and Jimmie Rodgers.

7.
Now, Mary had a little lamb,
  It had a sooty foot.
In little Mary's bread and jam
  His sooty foot he put.
            Chorus:

8.
A peanut sittin' on a railroad track,
  Its heart was all a-flutter.
The train came roarin' round a curve
  Toot, toot! Peanut Butter.
            Chorus:

9.
I went to see my Susie,
  She met me at the door,
Her shoes and stockings in her hand,
  And her feet all over the floor.
            Chorus:

10.
Oh! they tell me that a grave-yard
  Is a dawg-gone lonesome place,
They pull you down into a hole
  And throw mud in your face.
            Chorus:

imbalance in most cases. For every piece cited one could no doubt find two or three more which appear in both black and white tradition; but I think the selection gives a fairly comprehensive idea of common-stock material.

Why this shared repertoire should have existed is clear enough. In the first place, it is not in the nature of such songs and tunes to be segregatable, and, firm and ubiquitous though racial divisions may have been, they could not prevent – and probably few would have wished them to prevent – the use by blacks of white, or by whites of black material. And increasingly the concepts of 'this is a nigra song' and 'this is one o' them hillbilly pieces' would become unreal when applied to *John Henry*, say, or *Ain't Nobody's Business*. No doubt white musicians used to perform blues with a certain consciousness that they were 'nigger picking', and expressed this consciousness to their audience; the phenomenon is observable even today. But, as the reader will see, I have put no blues in the common-stock list, except a handful which differ significantly from the run of blues; they are basically unimprovised, and retain, through all their manifestations, tunes and at least a few verses which are peculiar to themselves. In some cases they even keep characteristics of performance, like *Poor Boy, Long Way From Home*, which is scarcely ever played without bottleneck or knife-style guitar accompaniment. (This is almost as true of *John Henry*.) Some later blues have the same 'fixed' structure, for instance *Key To The Highway* and *Milk Cow Blues*, but it would not be reasonable to call them common-stock pieces, for they are common only *within* the black tradition, not outside it, and when used in extra-traditional circumstances have a perceptible quality of conscious adaptation. White versions of *Milk Cow Blues*, for example, sound not like independent expressions of a traditional song, but like 'covers' of Kokomo Arnold's hit (02.1).

Then, as indicated earlier, almost every opportunity of building his repertoire came to the rural musician through omni-racial media. Tent shows may not have played to integrated audiences, but broadcasts and records could not be subjected to racist controls, except in so far as many blacks could not afford a radio or phonograph. And in the crowd at a carnival, or before a medicine show platform, though the black man might have to stand at the back, he was still in earshot of the music.

Again, it is easy to be swayed by the huge mass of blues and to suppose that they were always the dominant strain in the black tradition. But it is quite clear that the blues are a twentieth

Black (left) and white versions of the shared song Salty Dog, *recorded in 1924 and 1930 respectively.*

century music, even though their roots may be found in the 1880s and 1890s. If the black man had any form of leisure-time music in the nineteenth century, it probably belonged to this common stock. Which is not to say that black music was merely derivative; one can point to countless verses and tunes which bear a strong black stamp. The great quality of the common stock was adaptability; its great power, assimilation; it was neither black nor white, but a hundred shades of grey. And the evidence from twentieth century sources which suggests otherwise, which emphasises the divergent paths of the traditions, speaks to us not of the past but of the new century and its new mood. As the black man sought rights and equality, the tidily stratified society of the south was disrupted and the races drew apart. As if expressing this conflict of interests and of aims, the black and white musical traditions took different roads as well. The first decade of this century saw du Bois' *The Souls Of Black Folk* and the foundation of the NAACP; it also witnessed the earliest burgeonings of the blues.

But time is a tortoise in the south, and as late as the 'thirties we can find musicians who drew as much from the common stock as from the newer blues. Many of them were located round east Tennessee, Kentucky and the Virginias – one of the most fertile areas in which country music grew. A musician from those parts could reach, without much travel, into North Carolina, northern

Georgia and Alabama; the south-east was his oyster. A black could be one week in the mountains of east Tennessee, where his people were outnumbered twelve to one; next in Memphis or Atlanta or Birmingham, in ghettos which reversed the ratio. There are some artists, however, whose strong allegiance to older, shared forms suggests that they were most at home in the areas where blacks were scattered; such as Joe Evans and Arthur McClain, 'The Two Poor Boys'. Their extraordinary group of 1931 recordings includes a *Sitting On Top Of The World* (A17) based closely upon the Mississippi Sheiks' hit of the previous year, and a batch of blues; but also, as mandolin-guitar duets, *Sourwood Mountain* (A17), *Old Hen Cackle* (A17) and *John Henry* (A25); the 1927 'pop' *What Do I Care What Somebody Said?*, put over as *Take A Look At That Baby* (A17) with immense gusto and two kazoos; and, in *New Huntsville Jail* (A17), a lugubriously paced parody of another recent hit, the white Darby and Tarlton's *Birmingham Jail*. The choice of Huntsville, and the Birmingham location of their earlier recordings, suggests that the Two Poor Boys were from north Alabama or east Tennessee; one may also find somewhat abstruse similarities with Billy Bird (probably from Alabama) and Carl Martin, who moved from Virginia as a young boy to grow up in Knoxville. Brownie McGhee was born in that city, and his uncle – named John Evans, as it happens – was, according to Paul Oliver's gleanings, 'a fiddler who played in the hill country style which was characteristic of both Negro and white dance functions'.

Someone else who played for dances both sides of the colour line was the mandolinist Yank Rachell, who worked in the 'twenties in the Brownsville area of Heywood County, in west Tennessee. His book included *Bugle Call Rag* and *Turkey In The Straw*; and he also recalls *The Waltz You Saved For Me* and *You Are My Sunshine*, which is informative, for these were written in 1930 and 1940 respectively, so Rachell must have continued his white dance engagements as late as the Second World War; at which time he was very well established, as a blues singer and blues writer, on the black market.

While Rachell's mandolin work is strongly blues flavoured, the presence of that instrument in a black group generally brings a taste of white music. Coley Jones's Dallas String Band found much of its employment 'serenading' with *Shine*, *Hokum Blues* and the sparkling *Dallas Rag* (A33). This last is of interest as one of the few rural ragtime recordings; a couple of others were *Easy*

Winner (A26) and *Somethin' Doin'* (A17), by Nap Hayes and Matthew Prater, who, like Evans and McClain, used the mandolin-guitar duet form widely popular among white musicians, such as the Callahan, Shelton and Monroe Brothers. Hayes was probably exposed to ragtime when working with the pianist Cooney Vaughn, and he ably supported Prater's fluent mandolin runs. Both *The Easy Winners* and *Something Doing* (to give them their exact names) are by Scott Joplin; and this version of the latter composition was the only one to appear on record between the piano-roll era and the Second World War. The same would be true of *Easy Winner*, were it not that Hayes and Prater do not play this tune at all, but assemble under its name two strains from Joplin's *The Entertainer* and one from J. Bodewalt Lampe's *Creole Belles*. As it happens, this is the only record of *The Entertainer* from the cited period, too. *Creole Belles* was recorded by Mississippi John Hurt (23.1), soon after his reappearance in the musical world in 1963; his guitar treatment may be compared with a 1902 version, by banjoist Vess L. Ossman (A26).

The rest of the Hayes-Prater recordings had their surprises, for the pair was joined by Lonnie Johnson, singing and playing violin, and the trio rendered *I'm Drifting Back To Dreamland* and *Let Me Call You Sweetheart*, which one suspects Johnson sang; he readily produces numbers like these to this day. Neither performance, however, was issued, and the rags, with blues couplings, appeared only in the OKeh old time series, about the same time as the Mississippi Sheiks were being similarly marketed with *The Sheik Waltz* and *The Jazz Fiddler*. *Let Me Call You Sweetheart*, incidentally, has struck a responsive chord in other black breasts; Furry Lewis of Memphis still sings it (27.4). It was written in 1910, the birth-year of *Dill Pickles;* this rag too is much favoured by rural mandolinists and fiddlers.

If Lonnie Johnson's dulcet and musicianly fiddling reflects his years of work with lady blues singers in St Louis clubs, the coarse tone of Eddie Anthony suggests the rough and noisy working life of a street busker. Anthony was a member of Peg Leg Howell's Gang, a cheery Atlanta-based combination whose work has some affinities with the white music of north Georgia, as played by Fiddlin' John Carson, Earl Johnson and Gid Tanner's Skillet-Lickers. Everyone here drew on common stock; the Gang performed *Turkey In The Straw* – masked, on record, as *Turkey Buzzard Blues* – and *Tickle Britches* and *Tantalizing Bootblack*, while in the work of the leading white musicians there repeatedly

33

ERNEST THOMPSON

THE explosion, which years ago robbed Ernest Thompson of his eyesight, gave to the South one of its greatest minstrels. The visual power that was lost to him seems to have passed into the beauty and understanding of his singing. Ernest Thompson is claimed by all the South, although his native state is North Carolina. Thompson is master of the guitar and the harmonica, and, like other famous Southern minstrels, has the ability to play his own accompaniments.

occur tunes like *Ain't Nobody's Business*, *The Arkansas Traveler*, *Bully Of The Town* and *I Got Mine*.

Some of these are also to be found in the repertoire of Stovepipe No. 1, whose real name was the prosaic one of Sam Jones. He probably came from Cincinnati; he certainly took his nickname from the length of stovepiping which he blew in jug fashion. Playing guitar, and soloing alternately on the pipe and a harmonica, he recorded *Cripple Creek*, *Sourwood Mountain*, *Turkey In The Straw*, *Arkansas Traveler*, *Dixie Barn Dance*, *Dan Tucker* and several blues and religious numbers. His music was strikingly similar to that purveyed by the white harmonica-and-guitar one man bands – Walter Peterson, for instance, or Ernest Thompson, who played twenty-odd instruments, or George Reneau, 'The Blind Musician Of The Smoky Mountains'. Though an interesting figure, both for his material and for his early (1924) recording date, Jones played in a somewhat pedestrian fashion, less excitingly than, say, Daddy Stovepipe (Johnny Watson), who derived *his* name – it has been said – from the tall hat he wore; or, more plausibly, from his dark colouring. He claimed he was born in 1870, which made him an exact contemporary of Uncle Dave Macon; and he too made some records in 1924, playing guitar and harmonica, but he did not then show much white influence. When found in Chicago in 1960 by Paul Oliver, he had learned *Tennessee Waltz* and *South Of The Border*; no doubt he used the

Photograph: Daddy Stovepipe on Maxwell Street, 1960.

latter a good deal when he 'went down to Old Mexico, played some with them Mexican fellers' (Oliver: 1965). The sobriquet he part-shared with Sam Jones was strangely popular; there was also a Sweet Papa Stovepipe, who recorded a couple of vaudeville songs in 1926, and Stovepipe Johnson, who yodelled.

For songs of a more personal kind we may return briefly to Atlanta. Waymon 'Sloppy' Henry, who was associated with Peg Leg Howell's circle, sang a few semi-moralising pieces, such as *Canned Heat Blues*, about the effects of home-made alcohol, and *Bobbed Haired Woman Blues*, which reminds one of the popular white song *Why Do You Bob Your Hair, Girls?* He also declared that *The Best Cheap Car In The Market Is A Ford* – a favourite vaudeville theme, but one with surprising relevance to country musicians, for Henry Ford sponsored fiddling contests and even created his own record label for 'Henry Ford's Old Time Dance Orchestra' (see A50). Yet another theme which 'Sloppy' Henry touched upon was the topical tragedy; his *Royal Palm Special Blues* has connections, albeit slight ones, with the widely known *Wreck Of The Royal Palm*, one of the many compositions depicting railroad disasters. Quite why train crashes, child murders,

Carson Robison and some of his hits.   Right: Darwinism refuted, under a pseudonymous composer-credit.

Columbia

REG. U. S. PAT. OFF.

Columbia

The John T. Scopes Trial

(Carlos B. McAfee)

Solo-Guitar and Violin Accomp.

VERNON DALHART, Tenor

15037-D

(140680)

MADE AND PAT'D IN U.S.A. AUG. 11, '08. JAN. 21, '13 AND MAY 22, '23. COLUMBIA PHONOGRAPH COMPANY, INC., NEW YORK U.S.A.

robberies and assassinations should have been such popular subjects among southerners is hard to say; no doubt it was a development of the eighteenth and nineteenth century broadside tradition, which spawned so many Laments, Confessions and Last Speeches. Certainly the new disaster ballads were produced in much the same way, by professional song-mongers; now, however, unlike Catnach's hacks, they eschewed anonymity. The prolific Carson Robison described the process to a *Collier's* reporter in 1929: 'First, I read all the newspaper stories of, say, a disaster. Then I get to work on the old typewriter. There's a formula, of course. You start by painting everything in gay colours . . . that's sure-fire. Then you ring in the tragedy – make it as morbid and gruesome as you can. Then you wind up with a moral.' It certainly was sure-fire; Columbia's Frank Walker sold tens of thousands of copies of Robison's *The John T. Scopes Trial* (refrain: 'the old religion's better after all') in the courthouse

Victor

Tenor with violin and guitar

Death of Floyd Collins
(Andrew Jenkins)
Vernon Dalhart
19779–B

square of Dayton, Tenn., where it all happened. The Rev Andrew Jenkins ('Blind Andy'), an Atlantan Holiness preacher, did even better with *The Death Of Floyd Collins*, about a Kentuckian pot-holer who was trapped by a rock-fall and perished under the floodlights of journalistic ballyhoo in February 1925.

Such tragedies caused scarcely a flicker of interest in black musical circles; none of the ballads were recorded by blacks, and they were only very occasionally referred to; the Memphis Jug Band, for instance, make a half joking allusion to the Collins affair in their mainly sexual *Cave Man Blues* (A19). Whites might sing about national disasters; for the black man his private tragedy was more than enough inspiration. And when a black was caught up in some cataclysm, he pointed no moral; he simply mourned for himself and his family or friends. The Dixon Brothers sang of a *Wreck On The Highway*, and every verse tapered off into the moralist's sternly pointed finger: 'I saw the

Dorsey (left) and Howard Dixon.

wreck on the highway, but I didn't hear nobody pray.' The black singer looked at the overwhelming floods of 1927, and his concern was solely for the homeless and death depleted families. No talk of divine retribution. Is it too bold to see in the moralising songs of the white south an indirect expression of racial guilt?

Of course, it was possible to talk of your surroundings without dwelling on tragedy. Those north Georgian whites of whom we spoke above had an especial fondness for topical songs and discussions about moonshining, taxation and cotton prices; the Skillet-Lickers' fourteen-part saga of the *Corn Licker Still In Georgia* (pts. 9 and 10 on 42.1) was immensely well received. Possibly it was in an effort to popularise these skits with the black audience that Columbia had Barbecue Bob and his brother Charley Lincoln record a couple of double-sided 'happenings', *It Won't*

39

Be Long Now (pt. 1 on A7) and *Darktown Gamblin'*, but the Atlanta pair did little more than jive each other about their girlfriends in the former and quarrel over the dice in the other. There was no mention of the larger world of agricultural affairs and local politics, but this silence tells us less about the personalities of the brothers than about the suppression of free comment among southern blacks. A Tennessee farmer wrote in the middle of the nineteenth century, 'An employer should never ask a negro any questions whatever about the business of the plantation, or the condition of the crops; nor say anything in the presence of the negroes about the overseer, for they are always ready to catch any word that may be dropped, and use it if possible to cause a disturbance between the master and the overseer.' (Patterson: 1922).

If blacks were silent about agricultural work, they were not much more loquacious about other occupations. Many white singers found matter for dissatisfaction in the textile mills of Carolina

Photograph: Maybelle (left), A. P. and Sara Carter.

where they worked long and disagreeable hours for low wages; from these grim surroundings grew Dorsey Dixon's *The Weaver's Blues*, *Weave Room Blues* and *Spinning Room Blues*; Dave McCarn's *Cotton Mill Colic*; J. E. Mainer's *Hard Times In A Cotton Mill*. On their farms they had been 'white trash'; they joined the south's industrial revolution, filed into the mills, and found themselves labelled 'factory trash'. Black workers had little to say on this theme, though they praised the economic opportunities offered by the steel mills of Pittsburgh and Chicago. Coal-mining offered a slightly more productive seam of song; the shafts of Birmingham, Ala., were dug deep into Trixie Smith's *Mining Camp Blues* (1925) and Sonny Scott's *Coal Mountain Blues* and *Working Man's Moan* (1933). Alongside them we may place the Carter Family's celebrated *Coal Miner's Blues* (1938) (11.1) and the less well known *The Miner's Blues* (1928) of Frank Hutchison. Untypically, the black songs are more informative about the work:

> Oh, I went on Coal Mountain,
> > saw the men pulling coals from the mine;
> Lord, I went on Coal Mountain,
> > saw the men pulling coals from the mine;
> I saw the men wearing their mine lamps
> > where all the lights did shine.
> > > > > Sonny Scott, *Coal Mountain Blues*

> These blues are so blue, they are the coal black blues;
> For my place will cave in, and my life I will lose.
> > > > > Carter Family, *Coal Miner's Blues*

The Carters found their song on a collecting trip, in Lee County, Va.; it was locally popular in the mining community. Whether its composer was black or white we have no way of knowing; blacks were not numerous in the Virginias, but where they *were* to be found was in mining settlements. It is worth recalling that the Family often took a portable tape-recorder on their travels, in the form of one Leslie Riddles, a black singer/guitarist from Kingsport, Tenn. His job was to learn the tunes they collected, while A. P. Carter noted the words. Under his tuition, Maybelle picked up many of her instrumental ideas; and *Cannonball* came directly from him. Riddles had a friend in Brownie McGhee, who also lived in Kingsport during the 'thirties, and he too used to be visited by A. P. in search of songs.

Photograph: Frank Hutchison, 'The Pride Of West Virginia'.

Hutchison was probably a Virginian as well, possibly from Logan County. His repertoire seems to have been very broad; from the common stock came *Stackalee* (A14), *Railroad Bill*, *The Deal* and *K. C. Blues*, a bottleneck guitar rendering of the *John Henry* tune. (Another hidden *John Henry* is Riley Puckett's *Darkey's Wail* (A21), which the blind guitarist prefaces, rather incongruously, with the words 'I'm gonna play for you this time a little piece which an old southern darky I heard play, comin' down Decatur Street the other day, 'cause his good girl done throwed him down.') Hutchison was a stunning guitarist who probably heard black stylists; they seem to have something to do with his approach to

42

Railroad Bill and the bottleneck-accompanied *Logan County Blues* and *Cannon Ball Blues* (A9) (which is not unlike Furry Lewis's song of the same name, also with bottleneck guitar). His singing, too, especially in *Worried Blues* and *Train That Carried The Girl From Town*, has some of the emotional force of black music. These two performances, recorded in April 1927 and issued as a coupling, have been suggested by Malone's informants as the first steel-guitar recordings in country music. This is difficult to interpret; there is, after all, an important difference between a steel (-bodied) guitar and a guitar (whether steel-made or not) played with a steel (or knife, or bottleneck). Malone appears to mean the latter, but his case is insubstantial; in the first place, this kind of playing is to be found on Hutchison's debut recordings of *circa* November 1926 – earlier versions of the same two titles – and secondly there are several black examples which predate all Hutchison's output: by Sam Butler, for instance, and indeed by Blind Lemon Jefferson, whose *Jack O' Diamond Blues* (25.2 ,4) of May/June 1926 may well fill the required role.

Hutchison's versatility also embraced an automobile song, *The Chevrolet Six*; a cante-fable on the 'Titanic', widely different from the black treatments by 'Rabbit' Brown, Blind Willie Johnson and William & Versey Smith (A14); a musical description, on the harmonica, of *The C & O Excursion Train*; and various stock figures of country humour like *The Burglar Man*, *Johnny And Jane* and *Old Rachel*, who far outstripped the Good Wyf Of Bathe by getting married forty-nine times. But where he stands out most from white traditions of 'nigger picking' – and 'nigger singing' too – is in his rhythmic approach; he talks and sings across the beat in a way that is at first disconcerting but adds great impetus to the already complex musical progression. Nor do any of his blues employ the heavy 4/4 rhythm which underlay all Jimmie Rodgers' blue yodels, and thus much subsequent white blues playing.

Black musicians from 'Hutchison country' and its environs – that is, from the Virginias and Carolinas – exhibit an extremely satisfying mixture of black and white traditions. Julius Daniels' *Can't Put The Bridle On That Mule This Morning* (15.1) was very close to versions collected in the field years earlier; it is essentially one of the *This Morning*, *This Evening*, *So Soon* family. He also played *Crow Jane Blues* (A46), a venerable piece found in the repertoire of the Knoxville-based Carl Martin and Sam Butler from the Carolinas. Lil McClintock of Clinton, S.C., we know to

Photograph: Spark Plug Smith in 1933. He took his nickname from a famous racehorse.

have supplied material to a field researcher; *Delia* was collected from him in 1923. Seven years later he had a chance to record, and he sang *Furniture Man* and *Don't Think I'm Santa Claus* (both A38). The latter has segments of *Everybody Works But Father* and a coon-song refrain,

> Lindy, O Lindy, you sweeter than sugarcane;
> Lindy, Lindy, say you'll be mine;
> While the moon am a-shinin',
> And my heart am a-twinin',
> Meet me, dear little Lindy, by the watermelon vine.

which suggests that McClintock was out of the minstrel school. To the north, in Virginia, William Moore of Rappahannock played rags; and Luke Jordan, who worked round Lynchburg, sang *Traveling Coon* (A43) and *Look Up, Look Down*, the former a latter-day minstrel piece, also known as *Traveling Man* and so recorded by the fat medicine show singer Jim Jackson, the latter probably a variant of the ubiquitous *In The Pines/Black Gal* theme. His *Cocaine Blues* (A43), with a typically fluent guitar part, incorporated elements of the *Furniture Man* motif. Jordan was well remembered by Brown Pollard and Percy Brown, who played with him at black and white functions; for the latter, they report, the group's book took in *Turkey In The Straw*, *Mississippi Sawyer* and *Soldier's Joy*. A recording unit which captured Jordan in Charlotte, N.C., also documented fiddle-guitar tunes by Andrew and Jim Baxter (A37, A38, A43). The racial identity of this pair has been questioned; Andrew's fiddling indeed has the high off-key sound of north Georgia playing, but his brother's inter-jections sound black enough, and the high proportion of blues in their repertoire is quite untypical of white fiddlers.

Artists like these are often hard to pin down to an area. Julius Daniels sang a *Richmond Blues* (15.1) which may indicate Virginian provenance; *Richmond Virginia Blues* by Spark Plug Smith may do so as well, but guesswork becomes really hazardous here, for the piece is no more than an 'unissued' entry in the discographies. Smith's discography, though, is a fascinating one; it takes in *Sweet Evening Breeze*, *In A Shanty In Old Shanty Town* and *My Blue Heaven*. The last named is an engaging parody, sung in a light, dreamy voice with something of the throwaway quality of the white talking bluesmen.

Parody, of course, was ever a mainstay of the rural performer. One of its funniest exponents was Uncle Dave Macon. Born in Tennessee in 1870, Uncle Dave set up his 'Macon Midway Mule & Wagon Transportation Company' around the turn of the century, and became a familiar sight on his Woodbury-to-Murfreesboro run. A fun musician until about 1918, he was then spotted by a talent scout of Loew's theatre circuit, and entered show business; at his death in 1952 he had still not retired. It is astonishing to realise that Uncle Dave was fifty-four when he first entered a recording studio – and he was one of the first country musicians on disc at that. His huge repertoire thus in-cluded songs far older than many of those recorded even in the earliest 'twenties, and his role as a preserver of the tradition is of the first importance. Most of the vaudeville-turned-folk pieces which we have mentioned in preceding pages are to be found in his songbag: *Shout, Mourner, You Shall Be Free*, *Sho' Fly, Don't Bother Me*, *Rockabout My Saro Jane*, *Jordan Is A Hard Road To Travel* (31.1), *Comin' Round The Mountain*, and so forth. With his Fruit Jar Drinkers he made *Hold The Woodpile Down* (31.1), a variant of the piece which Sam Charters collected from the black Mobile Strugglers in Alabama in 1954, as *Raise A Rukus Tonight* (A13); and the Strugglers harmonised on the refrain in just the same way as Macon's supporters did. *Over The Road I'm Bound To Go* (31.1) was more or less *Feather Bed* (A16), as Cannon's Jug Stompers called it. There were blues, fiddle tunes transposed to the banjo, riverboat songs, lullabies, sentimental ballads. One of the latter stimulated Uncle Dave's most delightful

parody; 'Now I'll sing you a beautiful song,' he announces, 'that a highly educated aristocratic broken-down aristocracy old-maid school-teacher sang to a wealthy old bachelor that called on her one Sunday afternoon on her guitar – and the words are simply *beau*tiful . . .', and with that he goes into a crazily exaggerated *Nobody's Darling But Mine* which paints the prim schoolmarm's parlour overtures with hilarious fidelity. One gets no inkling of these joys from the record label, which simply lists *Two-In-One Chewing Gum* (31.1); the disc starts with that piece, but Uncle Dave moves, halfway through, into the other routine. This was one of his favourite techniques – a forerunner, indeed, of the extended-play, four-tune record. Oddly enough, the one black artist who did it at all frequently was a man who has other links with Uncle Dave Macon: the Texan songster Henry Thomas, who played guitar and panpipes on a list of tunes that includes *John Henry* (45.1), *Arkansas* (A33), *The Fox And The Hounds* (45.1), *Jonah In The Wilderness* (A45), *Shanty Blues* (45.1) and *When The Train Comes Along* (45.1) – *all* of which Macon recorded, virtually all earlier. Then there are the Maconesque medleys; *Arkansas* includes some of *Traveling Coon* and another song, while *Bob McKinney* (45.1) takes the listener through *Wasn't He Bad?*, *Take Me Back*, *Make Me A Pallet On the Floor* and *Bully Of The Town*, though admittedly the changes in direction are not always very clearly signalled by Thomas's guitar. His playing had a country dance flavour, never more than in *Old Country Stomp* (A15) with its dance calls, and in this, too, he echoed the Macon spirit. It is hard to dismiss the suspicion that the Brunswick company, for whom Thomas made all and Macon the bulk of his titles, was attempting a sort of comparative issue programme – Macon for the whites, Thomas for the race – but its advertisements make no reference to this, and the selling would have been on a subliminal level at best. Furthermore, Macon's discs appeared several years earlier (though they were reissued closer to Thomas's day); and of course the songs concerned were so old that Thomas need not have learned them from, nor even have heard, Macon's interpretations. It is curious all the same.

Sam McGee, with banjo-guitar, and Uncle Dave Macon, with 5-string banjo. Their duet recordings on these two instruments are unique in old time music. Sam and Kirk McGee met Uncle Dave in 1923; today, in their seventies, they keep his music alive in Opry programmes – on the few occasions when they get air-time.

Letting out the Blues

> I've got the worried blues, God, I'm feelin' bad.
> I got no one, tell my troubles to.
> I'm gonna build me a heaven of my own.
> I'm gonna give all good-time women a home.
> Now fare thee, my honey, fare thee.

Single statements, each repeated twice to make a three-line stanza. They might have been selected at random from any of the early text collections; in fact they comprise about half of *Texas Worried Blues* (45.1) by Henry Thomas, with whom we closed the last chapter. They show the blues at almost their most primitive; the lazy timelessness of the field holler has been lost, but the unconfined quality remains. The song could have had not eleven stanzas but fifty-one or a hundred and one; it is a close-up of the blues, a detail photograph from the whole blues landscape. In 1928, when Thomas was recorded, the form must have been not old-time but oldest-time; almost every singer, black and white, was experimenting with this marvellously elastic medium.

There was Blind Lemon Jefferson, also a Texan; more than a third of his recordings were made before ever Henry Thomas sat in front of a microphone, and from the start he forged blues with new words, clearly defined themes and carefully conceived accompaniments. His impact was immediate and tremendous. 'Up 'til then,' recalls the Kentucky mountain musician Roscoe Holcomb, 'the blues were only inside me; Blind Lemon was the first to "let out" the blues.' Hobart Smith of Saltville, Va., remembers seeing him about the beginning of World War I. 'It was along about that time that Blind Lemon Jefferson came through, and he stayed around there about a month. He stayed with the other colored fellows and they worked on the railroad there; he'd just sing and play to entertain the men in the work camp. I think that right about there I started on the guitar' (Smith: 1965). Echoes of Jefferson can be heard in Smith's *Six White Horses* and *Railroad Bill* (A27, A47), both of which he learned from the older man, and in *Graveyard Blues*. Smith was inspired as guitarist, Holcomb

48

rather as singer; the latter's high, penetrating voice has much of Lemon's acid tone. Hobart Smith had other experiences of black music: 'the first fiddle I ever heard in my life was when I was a kid. There was an old colored man who was raised up in slave times. His name was Jim Spenser. He played *Jinny*, *Put The Kettle On* and all those old tunes like that. And he would come up to our house and he'd play . . .' Leadbelly spoke of an old fiddler, too, 'Poor Howard . . . the first fiddler after Negroes got free, in slavery time.' His own association with Blind Lemon was particularly close, as his recollections and songs bear out.

Interviewing bluesmen who grew up in the 'twenties has a recurrent motif: guitarists nearly always cite Jefferson as the great formative influence, with occasional mention of Blind Blake and Lonnie Johnson. For all his formidable technique, Johnson was not popular among country whites, but Blake's quick fingered rags and delicately picked blues accompaniments were admired both sides of the colour line. The Kentuckian guitarist Asa Martin acknowledges his skill, while his fiddle-playing companion Doc Roberts can remember jamming with Blake in a hall adjoining the Paramount recording studio. One of Blake's sessions, in about

Photograph: Fiddling Doc Roberts' Trio.

Photograph: Brownie McGhee with jazzbo.

May 1927, was interspersed with titles by the Kentucky Thoro-
breds, and the discographers Dixon and Godrich note that 'it is
suggested that Blake may play on these'. Strangely enough, two
other instances of integrated recording sessions also bring in
Kentuckian musicians. The white singer Welby Toomey, recently
interviewed at his home in Lexington, recalled travelling up to the
Gennett studios in Richmond, Ind., with a black one-man bands-
man, Sammy Brown, also of Lexington. Brown, he said, had six

fingers on each hand, and played guitar, drums and so forth (Cohen, N.: 1969). Toomey's November 1927 recordings had guitar accompaniment, with occasional harmonica and 'jazzbow', and it sounds likely that Brown saw to all this. ('Jazzbow' I am taking to be a kazoo amplified with an old saxophone or trombone body; Brownie McGhee has such an instrument and gives it that name. Jazzbo Tommy Settles, too, was noted for his kazoo pyrotechnics. If the Gennett files mean literally a bow, that is a mouth-bow, like the ones used by the Ozark musicians Charley Everidge and Jimmie Driftwood, then Brown could not have done all the work, his extra fingers notwithstanding, for the mouth-bow, like the jew's harp, requires both hands.) Another local band was Taylor's Kentucky Boys, who employed a black fiddler named Jim Booker, but one would never guess his colour from the existing records.

White musicians did not listen only to the male black singers. Among Dock Boggs' most celebrated numbers are two from the 'classic blues' era, *Down South Blues* (A9) and *Mistreated Mama Blues* (A12). At a concert he prefaced a performance of *Down South Blues* as follows: 'this is one of the songs that I heard a colored girl sing; she'd sung it and recorded it a few years before that, accompanied by piano. I'd never heard any blues played on a banjo before.' At another time he remembered the 'colored girl' as Sara Martin, OKeh recording star of the early 'twenties, who did indeed make the original *Mistreated Mama Blues*, with piano, in 1923. *Down South Blues*, however, was not hers but Clara Smith's – also a piano-accompanied 1923 performance. Another 'ruralised' Clara Smith piece was *31st Street Blues* of 1924, which turned up six years later in stringband form, the work of the Leake County Revelers.

If Dock Boggs had looked into Sara Martin's work more closely he *would* have heard blues on a banjo, for she was often partnered by Sylvester Weaver playing that instrument. Weaver's accompanying ideas, however, remained stolidly pianistic, and they have dated far more than Boggs' vivid, unusually melodic conceptions. Dock had heard other black music sympathetically; 'there was a colored string band playing for a dance in Norton (his native town, in Virginia). I stuck my head in at the door and I liked the way the banjo-player played, so I said to myself, I am going to learn to play that way . . . ' (Boggs: 1964).

Another banjoist who learned from black sources was Sam McGee, a companion of Uncle Dave Macon and member of his

Fruit Jar Drinkers. Sam and his brother Kirk were born in Franklin, Tenn., and heard black street musicians early in their career; their playing, Sam recalls, 'would just ring in my head'. A black banjoist and guitarist called Jim Sapp had particular influence upon Sam McGee, who quickly became skilful at reproducing raggy 'nigger picking' styles. His *Easy Rider*, played on the six-string banjo-guitar, is a stunning performance, as is *Railroad Blues* (A9), a cleverly arranged and good-humoured

Left: Dock Boggs, 1927. Below: DeFord Bailey, c. 1928.

blues with guitar accompaniment. In it he plays a break which he introduces with 'here come DeFord Bailey now with the harmonica'. Bailey was a fellow performer on Grand Ole Opry, the one exception to the programme's unwritten colour bar; he represents, I suspect, genial patronisation rather than genuine musical interaction. It was he, according to one story, who opened the first Opry broadcast when he blew *Pan-American Blues* into the WSM microphone; he was definitely among the Opry men who made the first Nashville recordings, for Victor in September/October 1928. (Country-music historians have so far been unable to pinpoint the first performance recorded in Music City. It was

Photograph: this sentimental ballad by the Sheiks, the reverse side of Yodeling Fiddling Blues, *was issued in the 'race' series. A similar composition was* Too Long, *recorded by the Sheiks and – twice – by Charlie McCoy.*

the Binkley Brothers' Clodhoppers' *Watermelon Hanging On De Vine* of September 28, 1928.) Bailey today has a shoe-shine pitch in Nashville and puts too high a price on his services for any record company to engage him. No doubt he is justified; Opry contemporaries have reported that he was often not paid for his appearances. His few records (two are on A40) were issued largely in the old time listings. But he made at least one mark on a black listener; Sonny Terry remembers a visit Bailey made to his home area of Rockingham, N.C., and has enshrined the memory in a fine recording of Bailey's *Alcoholic Blues* (44.1).

We cannot leave Opry and its luminaries without one anecdote. A friend of his was talking one day to John Jackson, the fine black guitarist who is among the last decade's most pleasing discoveries. He recounted the story of DeFord Bailey and his unique position on Opry. John was puzzled. The only black artist? What about Uncle Dave Macon?

One wonders if John would have had any difficulties about the Mississippi Sheiks; as we have already mentioned, they were marketed as both race and old time artists. They came from the large and musical Chatman family of Jackson, Miss.; most of the eleven brothers who grew up in the 'teens and 'twenties could play at least one instrument. Bo Chatman was to attain fame as the dirtiest, and funniest, blues singer on the Bluebird label, but he played guitar and fiddle as a member of the Sheiks from 1930 to 1935, along with his brothers Lonnie (vocal and fiddle) and Sam (vocal and guitar) and their friend Walter Vincent, or Vincson (vocal, guitar and fiddle). Another prominent musical family in Jackson were the McCoys, Joe – who married Memphis Minnie – and Charlie. Between all these men there was much interaction, and they produced a large set of splinter-group recordings. Their most popular kind of music, on discs, was a verse / refrain blues, generally with a sexually metaphorical title: *Driving That Thing* (the Sheiks' first recording), *Pencil Won't Write No More*, *Loose Like That* (an answer, of course, to *It's Tight Like That*), *Your Friends Gonna Use It Too* (a two-sider), *It Is So Good* (another), and so on. There were some topical pieces, like Bo's Depression-era coupling with Charlie McCoy, *Mississippi I'm Longing For You* backed with *The Northern Starvers Are Returning Home*; the latter was to the tune of *Corrine Corrina*, a common-stock song the pair had recorded two years before. Then Charlie did *Times Ain't What They Used To Be*, which brother Joe followed with *The World Is A Hard Place To Live In*. Bo also sang the startlingly titled *The Yellow Coon Has No Race*, unfortunately never issued, and a charming *Good Old Turnip Greens*.

When I was a little bird, I always wanted to fly;
I flapped my wings like a seagull and I flew up to the
         sky;
When I got up in heaven, I seen somethin' I never have
         seen;
There was a lot of curly-headed coons just a-scratchin'
         on the turnip greens.
   He's a fool about his turnip greens, oh, yes indeed he
         are!
   Corn bread and buttermilk, and the good old turnip
         greens.

Mister Spencer went to Chicago, and I went to New Orleans;
I got mad and walked all the way back home just to get
         my greasy turnip greens;
Oh, the white man wears his broadcloth, and the Indian
         he wears jeans;
But here comes the darky with his overalls on, just
         a-scratchin' on the turnip greens.
   He's a fool about his turnip greens, oh, yes indeed he
         are!
   Corn bread and it's greasy, and the good old turnip
         greens.

White man goes to the college, and the Negro to the
         fields;
The white man learns to read and write, and the nigger
         will learn to steal;
Oh, the white folks in their parlours, just eatin' their
         cake and cream;
But the darky's back in the kitchen, just a-scratchin' on
         the turnip greens.
   He's a fool about his turnip greens, oh, yes indeed he
         are!
   Corn bread and pepper sauce, and the good old turnip
         greens.

It reads like a minstrel song with sharpened points. Perhaps it was a parody of a non-racial original; versions without the 'darky'

Photograph: the Sheiks, c. 1930 – Bo Chatman, Walter Vincson, Sam Chatman.

lines have been recorded by whites like Pie Plant Pete and the Massey Family. Some of the phrases crop up in contemporary blues, like the parlour / kitchen couplet in Jefferson's *Piney Woods Money Mama* (25.2, 3) of 1928. Probably the piece was put together, like so many black and white songs, from both minstrel and folk sources.

A more successful Chatman production was the Sheiks' *Stop And Listen Blues* (A54). Strongly reminiscent of the Jackson bluesman Tommy Johnson, it took its catchy title from the warning notice 'Stop – Look – Listen' on ungated level-crossings. Kokomo Arnold's 1935 *Stop Look And Listen* (02.1) came nearer to the phrase, but was solidly based on the work of Johnson and the Chatmans; most other versions came directly from the Sheiks' hit, among them probably William Hanson's late 1930 recording. On the other side of this disc, Hanson – who was white – sang *Sitting On Top Of The World*, the original of which was, like *Stop And Listen Blues*, made at the first Sheiks session in February 1930. *Sitting* (A37), the group's biggest seller, was a slow 8-bar blues, easy to learn and infinitely adaptable; its name was a defiant assertion of well-being,

57

but its pace was usually funereal, and the odd clash probably added to the song's appeal. The Western Swing bands of the 'thirties grabbed it enthusiastically, and there were versions by Leon's Lone Star Cowboys (1932), Milton Brown and his Brownies (1934) and Bob Wills' Texas Playboys (1935). Black popularity has been constant from the obvious 'cover' by the 'Alabama Sheiks' in 1931 to the 1950s discs by Brownie McGhee & Sonny Terry and Howlin' Wolf. Slight revampings have been frequent – for instance, McGhee & Terry's *Better Day* (44.2) – and the framework of the song is now established as a blues standard.

It is possible that the Sheiks intended the song to be a comment, of a sort, upon the earlier popular number, *I'm Sitting On Top Of The World* (*Just Rolling Along*), which emerged in 1925 and moved with an altogether more lively gait. (In the same year and from the same writers – Lew Brown, Ray Henderson and Sam M. Lewis – came *Five Foot Two, Eyes Of Blue*, which the Sheiks also played; 'in '28,' Sam Chatman told Paul Oliver, 'we got to playin' up at Leroy Percy Park for the white folks all the week. *Eyes of Blue*, that's what we played for white folks. *Dinah*, that's another . . .') From more traditional backgrounds came *Bootleggers' Blues* (12.1), which embraced lines documented many years before by collectors, and *Honey Babe Let The Deal Go Down*, the gambling song which virtually everyone knew, from Peg Leg Howell to Charlie Poole (35.1). These are airs from the common stock, but others of the Sheiks' songs betrayed one-way white influence, such as *Yodeling Fiddling Blues* (A35). This was a neat marriage of blues fiddling and blue yodelling, and thus capitalised on country music's most exciting new sound. 'Go and learn to yodel,' singer Walter Vincson urged his hearers, while a Chatman fiddle moaned behind him; 'that's the way to win a home.' One like the $50,000 'Yodeler's Paradise', perhaps, which marked the top of the ladder for the creator of this new sound: 'America's Blue Yodeler' – Jimmie Rodgers.

04261	SITTING ON TOP OF THE WORLD	Light Crust Doughboys
	(Three Shif-Less Skonks)	
03139	SITTIN' ON TOP OF THE WORLD	Bob Wills & Texas Playboys
	(Black and Blue Rag)	

| { I'm Sitting on Top of the World | Frank Crumit } | 19928 | 10 | .75 |
| { Sweet Child (I'm Wild About You) | Gene Austin } | | | |

'That's the idea of the white people'

Much is made, in blues-collecting circles, of the Mississippi men – Charley Patton and Son House, Robert Johnson and Tommy McClennan, Muddy Waters and John Lee Hooker; the list runs into dozens. They are singers of sometimes frightening emotional power, and, if they are not – as some would have them – the creators of the blues, they certainly represent one of its most passionate strains. The man whose efforts crystallised the white blues form and ensured its future in country music was a Mississippian too. Jimmie Rodgers was born in Meridian in 1897, the son of an M & O gang foreman, and his father's work took the pair (his mother died early) to many southern cities. Rodgers' musical environment has often been described; how he fetched water for the black gandy dancers in the Meridian yards; how he heard their songs and slang, and was taught the banjo by them. He travelled the line between his home town and New Orleans, as flagman or brakeman, and must often have met itinerant musicians looking for a free ride. Perhaps, musician himself, he gave them room in exchange for a song or a tune. (Listen to Jimmie Davis' 1931 recording *The Davis Limited* [A51]. Davis, narrating the events of a southern railroad journey, adopts the role of brakeman to ask a guitar-carrying hobo 'say, boy, can you play that thing?' 'Well, I can kind of strum a few tunes on it,' comes the reply. 'Let's have it, boy,' says Davis; 'if you can play that thing, you ride this train. Otherwise, you hit the ground.' 'Well, boy,' returns the hobo thankfully, 'I'm headed for home and here's your number.') Rodgers' career on the tracks was curtailed by tuberculosis in 1925, and he took up, full time, the musical life which he had for some years enjoyed as an amateur. His repertoire already included popular dance tunes, which he learned as rhythm guitarist in a local 'sweet' stringband, and blues, picked up from black musicians on Meridian's Tenth Street; and he branched out into minstrelsy when he became a blackface singer in a travelling medicine show.

Illustrations: Jimmie Rodgers. Right: Rodgers' Entertainers (Jimmie rear left, with tenor banjo).

(Clarence Ashley was playing the same part in a Bristol, Tenn.-based company as late as the middle 'fifties.) Moving to Asheville, N.C., for the mountain air, Rodgers secured a radio engagement in early 1927; a quartet composed of himself, Jack Pierce and the Grant Brothers was billed as the 'Jimmie Rodgers Entertainers'. In July he heard of Ralph Peer's talent-seeking trip to Bristol and travelled there to see if Victor could use him. On August 4 he made his first recordings.

RODGERS, JIMMIE

JIMMIE RODGERS

Born into a family of railroaders, at Meridian, Miss., Jimmie Rodgers, when little more than a child, went to work on the road as a common laborer. Curiously enough, the music which was to cause his rise to affluence, began simultaneously with his first employment. The old songs and ballads of the railroad, some born of pioneer toil on the railroads, some the crooning songs of the hoboes who were attracted to the new railroads like crows to a farmer's fence —these constituted the music that Jimmie Rodgers first knew. He learned to play the guitar, and to sing in a naturally appealing voice the songs of the road. Later Jimmie became a brakeman but his health failed. He wandered about the country, his guitar and his, voice providing the necessities of life.

A Victor recording expedition into the mountains of Tennessee discovered Jimmie Rodgers, quite accidentally. From the first impromptu recording, Jimmie's Victor records have been tremendously successful. He is now a headline vaudeville artist, and his Victor success grows greater with each succeeding record.

RECORDS BY JIMMIE RODGERS

Away Out On the Mt. 21142	Desert Blues V-40096	My Little Old Home 21574
Ben Dewberry's	I'm Lonely and	My Old Pal 21757
Final Run 21245	Blue V-40054	Never No Mo' Blues 21531
Blue Yodel 21142	I'm Sorry We Met 22072	Sailor's Plea, The V-40054
Blue Yodel—No. 2 21291	In the Jailhouse	Sleep Baby Sleep 20864
Blue Yodel—No. 3 21531	Now 21245	Soldier's Sweetheart 20864
Blue Yodel—No. 4 V-40014	Lullaby Yodel 21636	Treasures Untold 21433
Blue Yodel—No. 5 22072	Memphis Yodel 21636	Waiting for Train V-40014
Brakeman's Blues 21291	Mother Was a Lady 21433	

Blind Alfred Reed A. G. Karnes

It was a momentous stay for the Victor team, since they also captured the Carter Family (A. P., Sara and Maybelle), who, with Rodgers, were to subsidise the company through the Depression years. Musically, the twelve days in Bristol were amazingly rewarding; there were sessions by Ernest Stoneman and the Johnson Brothers, Henry Whitter and Blind Alfred Reed; the tremendous gospel singer Alfred Karnes, from Corbin, Ky.; a superb black harmonica player named El Watson, accompanied by Charles Johnson of the Brothers – another integrated session; and many other historic banjoists, fiddlers and stringbands. Rodgers' two pieces were moderately successful, and he was invited to come to Victor's Camden, N.J., studios in November. The session there was a watershed in country music history, producing the undying *Blue Yodel* ('T for Texas') (37.3b).

'The identifying characteristics of the "blue yodel",' John Greenway has written, 'are (1) the slight situational pattern, that of a "rounder" boasting of his prowess as a lover, but ever in fear of the "creeper", evidence of whose presence he reacts to either with threats against the sinning parties or with the declaration that he can get another woman easily enough; and (2) the prosodic pattern, the articulation of Negro maverick stanzas dealing with violence and promiscuity, often with double meaning, and followed by a yodel refrain.' This is true enough of many of Rodgers' thirteen blue yodels, and associated pieces like *Memphis Yodel* (37.4), though generally the boasting rounder takes second place to the rejected lover. An exception, in which the fear of rivalry is quite absent, is – oddly – *Jimmie Rodgers' Last Blue Yodel* (37.3a), a jaunty composition recorded only eight days before his death.

Striking features of the blue yodels include the very frequent railroad references. 'I can get more women than a passenger train can haul'; 'I've got my ticket, I'm sure gonna ride this train, / I'm goin' some place where I won't hear them call your name'; 'Look-a-here, Mister Brakeman, don't put me off your train, / 'Cause the weather's cold and it looks like it's goin' to rain'. If one did not know the man's early life one could still guess its railroad associations. Then there are the 'Negro maverick stanzas dealing with violence and promiscuity': 'Won't you tell me, mama, where you stayed last night ? / 'Cause your hair's all tangled and your clothes

JIMMIE RODGERS

JIMMIE RODGERS ◇ ◇

This record (No. 22488) An-
niversary Blue Yodel and
Any Old Time is of interest
because it marks the third
year during which this popular artist has been on the
Victor roster. Several years
ago a Victor representative
chanced to hear Rodgers
sing. He was playing his own
accompaniment and punctuating the texts of his songs
with the yodeling that has become a part of his vocaliz-
ing. The tremendous appeal . . . the home-y quality of
the voice and personality behind it . . . that those
songs expressed impressed the Victor man. And as a
result everybody can enjoy Jimmie's singing, and his
personality, too, for it is evident in his many records.
Listen to these two songs . . . you'll like them both!

don't fit you right', in *Blue Yodel No. 3* (37.4), comes two verses before 'I hate to see this evening sun go down, / 'Cause it makes me think I'm on my last go round' – and both verses are so common in black blues that it is unnecessary to cite examples. Or there is that beautifully concise couplet, 'When a man's down and out, you women don't want him round; / But when he's got money he's the sweetest thing in town', which was still in use in 1950; Baby Face Leroy Foster put it into his moving *My Head Can't Rest Anymore*. Another recurrent element is the city of Memphis, and it may be that Rodgers picked up some ideas from black singers there. 'I woke up this mornin', the blues all around my bed', from *Memphis Yodel*, is a favourite Furry Lewis line, and there are street references in *Blue Yodel No. 9* (37.3a), in which piece Rodgers was accompanied by Louis Armstrong and Earl Hines. Lewis also adapted the famous 'T for Texas, T for Tennessee' line to make 'M for Memphis, B for Birmingham' (*Skinny Woman*, 27.4). The connections are tenuous; lines used by Rodgers in this group of songs occur in several areas, and they were often recorded by Memphis singers because a lot of Memphis singers made records. On the other hand, Jimmie's medicine show tours must have taken him to the city; on one such trip he worked on the same bill as Memphian singer/guitarist Frank Stokes, and was remembered for it as far west as Fort Worth, Texas. Whether or not he had much truck with the Memphians, he heard plenty of south Mississippian black music on his Meridian-to-New Orleans trips. One of the last titles he recorded was a *Mississippi Delta Blues* (37.2), and *Mississippi River Blues* (37.5) was a touching evocation of those muddy waters. But like every artist with an acute commercial sense (or a good manager) he sold himself to as wide an audience as possible, with *Jimmie's Texas Blues* (37.2), *Peach Pickin' Time Down In Georgia* (37.3a), *My Little Old Home Town In New Orleans* (37.2), *Roll On Kentucky Moon* (37.5), *In The Hills Of Tennessee* (37.7), *My Carolina Sunshine Girl* (37.3b) and – a blanket coverage of his southern market – *Somewhere Down Below The Dixon Line* (37.2). Of course, the undeniable magic of these regional titles further sold the records to Rodgers' fans in England and Australia, India and Ireland, even Japan. (Nearly all his discs appeared in England and Australia during the 'thirties).

The blue yodels were a foundation upon which countless white country singers built. Their great strength lay partly in their similarity to, partly in their difference from black blues. Some whites would sing the blues in very black fashion, though few

Photograph: a scarce Zonophone 'International' issue, pressed in England for export. The 'three songs' were excerpts from Train Whistle Blues, Blue Yodel *and* Everybody Does It In Hawaii, *each piece having a different run-in point on the circumference of the disc.*

imitated the vocal tone and speech patterns deceptively well. Other singers may have found such re-creation unacceptable. For them the blue yodel, as a vehicle of blues feelings, was an attractive compromise. The 12-bar structure was fashionable, easily manipulated and aesthetically satisfying; the yodel drew listeners who had heard Swiss virtuosi on travelling shows; and the Hawaiian guitars which Rodgers and many of his successors often added caught a third section of the market. The style was a very happy compendium of popular rural motifs.

But one must not distort Jimmie Rodgers' work; his blues, blue yodels and blues-like songs were only a part of his repertoire.

The first two sessions, for example, had all the diversity which was and is typical of white country music. *Sleep, Baby, Sleep* (37.4) was an old lullaby (which the black vaudeville singer Charles Anderson recorded, with yodelling, in 1923); *The Soldier's Sweetheart* (37.5) was a reworked ballad. *Mother Was A Lady* (*If Brother Jack Were Here*) (37.7) was a popular song of 1893, while *Ben Dewberry's Final Run* (37.2) came from the hand of the Reverend Andrew Jenkins, of *Death Of Floyd Collins* fame. By songs of this kind as much as the bluer ones, Rodgers' memory was kept alive amongst his own people. The Western Swing bands of the 'thirties were great fans of his work; Bob Wills' Texas Playboys, for instance, successfully remade many Rodgers tunes, from *Gambling Polka Dot Blues* – Jimmie's original of which (37.7), with its solo piano accompaniment, had a touch of the vivacious female blues style – to the Depression-inspired *Never No More Hard Times Blues* (A23).

Black interest took many forms. First, there were textual reminiscences. The opening stanza of his *Waiting For A Train* (37.1) turned up in Peg Leg Howell's *Broke And Hungry Blues* (A7) and *Away From Home* (A38), both made some six months after Rodgers' song was recorded; and a verse from *Blue Yodel No. 4* (37.1), the reverse side of *Waiting For A Train*, appeared in *Broke And Hungry Blues* too. The whole of *Waiting For A Train* has been recorded by Snooks Eaglin (17.1) and Furry Lewis (27.4); Furry's version – which he calls *The Dying Hobo* – includes the yodel, which he introduces with 'I'm gonna try somethin' now – I may make a failure'. (He does. However, he is over seventy, and as a young man may have been more accurate.) That 'T for Texas' line which we have mentioned also cropped up in Frank Stokes' *Nehi Mama Blues* (40.1) of 1928, neatly elaborated:

Ah, now, T for Texas, T for Tennessee,
S is a mighty bad letter for she *s*tole away from me . . .

– and it was still recalled by J. B. Lenoir in 1960 (A11). Small borrowings, but they show that blacks listened to Rodgers' records. Some may even have regarded him as an honorary Negro; he certainly had ways which his acquaintances thought rather black, as Cliff Carlisle recounted to Eugene Earle: 'He crossed that leg – well, his leg didn't do like mine does; *my* leg won't hang down . . . he put one leg over the other, and it was hangin' right down . . .

Photographs: Jimmie Rodgers. Left: still from his movie The Singing Brakeman.

And he opened that mouth – and he had a long face, you know, long jaw, like; anyhow, it just flopped! Jimmie, he reminded me more of a colored person, or a negro, or whatever you want to call 'em . . . (another voice: "he played that part a whole lot") . . . than anybody I ever saw, in a way. He had that old southern, long southern drawl, you know . . .'

Though black singers might borrow from Rodgers' recordings, yodel – with a few exceptions – they could or would not. They had a similar device, however, in the falsetto. The voice was raised an octave, generally in the last syllable of a word, often at the end of a line; the effect was rather of a whoop or howl than of the see-sawing about the voice's breaking point which makes a yodel. It is difficult to tell what relationship there was between the two devices. David Evans has suggested, very reasonably, that the blue yodel synthesised Swiss (yodelling) and African (falsetto) traditions; the falsetto 'leap' was established among blacks since the days of the field holler – consider Vera Hall's *Wild Ox Moan* – and Rodgers, hearing it, thought it analogous to the yodel and inserted both into his blues. His minstrel experience may have helped too; yodelling was heard from blackface 'coons' as far back as 1847, when one Tom Christian introduced it on a Chicago stage. The full version of *Lily of Laguna* has a yodelled chorus.

Evans has investigated the late Jackson bluesman Tommy Johnson, whose trademark the falsetto 'leap' was, and he reports that Jackson-based singers like Ishman Bracey and Rubin Lacy saw Rodgers often in the 'twenties; it is interesting to speculate on the interchange between the white singer and Johnson's 'school'. Chester Burnett, whose powerful whooping owed a little to Johnson, claims he met Rodgers in the 'twenties and was given by him the nickname of 'Howlin' Wolf' which he has used ever since.

Among the other Mississippians through whom Evans has traced various threads of blues history was Skip James of Bentonia, not far out of Jackson. Skip's *Yola My Blues Away* (also known as *Four O'Clock Blues*) was sung – like all his material – entirely in falsetto; apparently blacks use 'yodeling' or 'yolaing' to denote both the techniques. Evans also recorded him singing *Waiting For A Train*. Yet another singer in this area was John Hurt, who sang an occasional Rodgers number in his latter-day stage act. Hurt first recorded through the recommendation of two white musicians in his home town of Avalon, Willie Narmour and Shell Smith. This fiddle-and-guitar duo had a longer recording career than Hurt, thanks chiefly to their *Carroll County Blues* hit (A9).

The sympathetic listener will find, I think, that Rodgers was a very great artist, and men of that stature, given a certain amount of circulation, do tend to cross social barriers; witness the impact of Blind Lemon. His delicate though masculine baritone could draw the best from a song, whether it was sentimental, like *Old Pal Of My Heart* (37.1), mournful, as in *Why Should I Be Lonely?* (37.6), gay – *My Little Lady* (37.1), *Everybody Does It In Hawaii* (37.6) – or resolute and self-assured, like some of the blues. There were pieces about *Daddy And Home* (37.1) and *Hobo Bill's Last Ride* (37.2), but Rodgers scarcely ever yielded to gross sentiment, and his tragic ballads have a refreshing simplicity and control. As if rejecting the formula ridden disaster songs of Robison & Co., he ended his buoyant version of *Frankie And Johnny* (37.4) with the words 'this story has no moral, this story has no end,/ This story just goes to show that there ain't no good in men . . .'

When the blue yodels caught on, both citybillies, like the

Illustrations: a best-selling commemorative record (top); the Rodgers Memorial in Meridian, flanked by Bill (left) and Charlie Monroe; and an English advertisement of 1935 – two years after his death.

prolific and polypseudonymous Frankie Marvin, and countrymen – Riley Puckett, for one – recorded songs in the new form. Puckett for some years attended the State Blind School in Macon, Ga., and while there he may have encountered the black singer Willie McTell, who was a pupil from 1922 to 1925. It may even have been McTell from whom he learned his interpretation of *John Henry*. Blind Willie enjoyed a long recording career, but had returned to street busking when he was found by folklorist John A. Lomax in November 1940. In an Atlanta hotel room he talked to Lomax about the development of the blues (32.3).

'I'm talking about the days of years ago – count from 1908 on up, to the 'riginal years. Back in the years of those days blues had started to be original, in 1914. From then until the war time, people always had times – from blues on up to original blues. Then on up to 1920 – the changed blues. After then there was more blues. After then there come the jazz blues – some like this . . . And after then there's more blues – come to fast pieces . . . And after then it come the blues of changed things – gettin' in the alley low. People call it the alley, calls it in the colored race of blues. Now we take our white race of the southern states; they plays a little different from we colored people. Now here's some of their pieces . . . That's the idea of the white people. Now you come back to the colored; they have a different type of playing. Now we have some pieces goes like this . . . now that's the colored. Here's our colored again . . . And still we have still down in the alley of blues, just like the white, when they play their yodelin' songs. But we have our blues, a little different – I thinks.'

McTell illustrates his points now and then with tune fragments on his resonant 12-string guitar; unfortunately he didn't have time to give any very good idea of the tunes' identities, though the 'colored' excerpts can be tracked down, for the most part, to various of his earlier commercial recordings. He appears to think that the bluest of the white blues are their 'yodelin' songs', and he may have had Rodgers in mind, but there was music closer to his home which had the essence of the blue yodel with a more searching emotional strength. It was provided by Tom Darby and Jimmie Tarlton, who had a resounding success with their second release, *Columbus Stockade Blues* and *Birmingham Jail*. The refrain of the former, 'Go and leave me if you wish to, / Never let me cross your mind; / In your heart you love some other, / Leave me, darling, I don't mind', came from an old Irish song, and can be heard even now from English traditional singers. *Birmingham Jail* was also a

70

Darby and Tarlton

reworking of an old theme, but it derived its particular success, apparently, from the fact that both artists had done time in that prison, and were felt to be singing from the heart. The pair's early recordings owe little to black song, the darkest element being Tarlton's steel guitar playing, which he says he taught himself before ever seeing Hawaiian guitarists, let alone black ones. Its lyrical figures nevertheless have a Hawaiian air rather than any other, but in some performances Tarlton shows considerable knowledge of black phrasing. His singing was always excellent, and attained a depth of feeling in their blues which was rarely matched among white country singers. *Traveling Yodel Blues* and *Touring Yodel Blues* indicate a fellowship with Rodgers; *Heavy Hearted Blues* and *Slow Wicked Blues* are fragmentary pieces which sound wholly improvised. Probably the recording director simply asked for 'some blues', as much for the lightning guitar work as for the words, and was rewarded with off-the-cuff performances. The duo were not primarily bluesmen, and a lot of the songs they called blues were only loosely so – *The Weaver's Blues*, for instance, which Tarlton learned from Dorsey Dixon when the two were working in the East Rockingham, S.C., textile mills. However, Jimmie has recorded some earthy items; *Ooze Up To Me* is a bouncy song-with-refrain out of the Mississippi Sheiks' mould, and he still plays a speedy *Red Hot Daddy Blues* along similar lines. He is as likely, though, to play *Vaya Con Dios* or *Sidewalks Of New York* or *Old Black Joe*; eclecticism is the spirit of his music.

One of Darby and Tarlton's records had an odd sequel. *Black Jack Moonshine* (April 1929) was a piece of some antiquity; White, who quotes a black version heard in North Carolina, says that it 'is related to a song of the white people, the tune and a few words of which I can remember from my childhood'. (He was born in 1892). His text has a refrain beginning 'coon shine, ladies, coon shine', which seems to refer to the 'coonjine' dance popular in the 1870s. Darby and Tarlton's tune has an appropriately jerky rhythm – 'coonjining' was a sort of shuffling – but they change the key word to 'moonshine' for a joke. There were jokes galore eight months later when Tampa Red, Georgia Tom and female impersonator Frankie 'Half-Pint' Jaxon gathered in a Chicago studio to record – under the sobriquet of 'The Black Hillbillies' – *Kunjine Baby*. Its tune was very close to the white pair's, but they stuffed the piece with comic stories and puns.

> 'Well, say, boy!'
> 'What?'
> 'You know, I feel kinda sick!'
> 'What you been eatin'?'
> 'Oh, I ain't been eatin' nothin' but eggs.'
> 'You got egg-zema!'

Is this true to the spirit of the medicine shows? Probably it is. Here is another of the trio's routines:

> 'What is all that round your mouth there?'
> 'You talkin' 'bout on my upper lip? That's my mustache!'
> 'Oh, beg pardon! Look like you swallowed a mule and left his tail stickin' out!'

And that particular joke was also told on record by Uncle Dave Macon (*I've Got The Mourning Blues*, 31.2).

Interviewer Norm Cohen has reported that Jimmie Tarlton 'feels strongly that the treatment of Negroes in the south is unjust and not according to God's intentions. He feels that the troubles the whites in the south are now having are their punishment for many years of mistreatment of Negroes.' (Cohen, N. & A. in 1966).

Blind Willie McTell found it difficult to explain to John Lomax why he had no 'songs about colored people havin' hard times there in the south'. 'Why,' asked Lomax, 'is it a mean world to live in?' 'Well, I don't know,' said McTell; 'it's not altogether. It has reference to everybody.' 'It's as mean for the whites as it is for the blacks. Is that it?' 'That's 'bout it.' It must have been difficult for even so experienced a field collector as Lomax to elicit unfettered replies from his black informants on this topic; certainly McTell sounds very uncomfortable in the conversation. But it was quite true that, economically, it was as mean a world for the whites, in many parts of the south, as for the blacks. (And in some northern areas too). Economic and social lowliness or deprivation are not the only qualifying ingredients of the blues, but they are important, and in songs about poor living standards there is considerable similarity in black and white treatments. Jimmie Tarlton's New Deal *Administration Blues* (43.1), with its closing stanza

> So hold up your head now,
>   Come fall in our line;
> We're gon' elect Franklin D. Roosevelt
>   For a mighty long time,

chimes in the same tone as, say, Champion Jack Dupree's *God Bless Our President*. McTell, too, had a Roosevelt song:

> Roosevelt is a mighty fine man, darlin', (*twice*)
> Roosevelt is a mighty fine man,
> Got to be president of our land, darlin'.

> Moonshine been here long enough, darlin', (*twice*)
> Moonshine been here long enough,
> Let's get right and drink up this stuff, darlin'.

> I got a gal in the white folks' yard, darlin', (*twice*)
> I got a gal in the white folks' yard,
> She don't drink liquor but she do play cards, darlin'.

The structure is that of an old song sometimes called *Sweet Thing*, collected from Mississippi blacks in 1909 as beginning 'What makes a Frenchman grow so tall, sugar-babe?'; perhaps more to the point, both the pattern and a similar melody had recently been used on a recording by the white singer Bill Cox, a topical one at that: *N. R. A. Blues*. Cox – who also celebrated

SMITH'S CHAMPION
HOSS HAIR
PULLERS, DR.

Going Down the River
In the Garden Where Potatoes
Just Give Me the Leavings
Nigger Baby
Save My Mother's Picture
Up in Glory

Smith's Hoss Hair Pullers

F. D. R.'s re-election in 1936 with *Franklin D. Roosevelt's Back Again* (A22) – used the repetitive little *Sweet Thing* tune to put over a unionist message – 'When you all join the N.R.A., we'll all feel happy and we'll all feel gay' – which would never have appeared in a black song. McTell's version, incidentally, went out under the title *Hillbilly Willie's Blues* (A43), which shows us the progress of the stratification imposed by recording companies (and perhaps record-buyers too) upon the old common stock.

We have already looked at the 'nigger'/'white man' antithesis of *Good Old Turnip Greens*; another stanza sometimes found in this song ran

> White man in the parlor reading latest news,
> Negro in the kitchen blacking Roosevelt's shoes.

And a more popular contrast was incorporated in the song of which this is a fragment:

> Well, a white lady smells like toilet soap,
> A yaller gal tries to do the same;
> But a poor black gal smells just like a ram billy goat –
> But she's smelling just the same!

The refrain to this gives the piece its commonest titles, *Charmin' Betsy* and *Do, Lord, Remember Me*; it appears to have started life as a parody of the spiritual with the latter name. In white hands it was often a fiddle or banjo breakdown, but the salty words occur in both race and hillbilly records, such as the Delta Boys' *Black Gal Swing* or Clarence Ganus' *All Night Long*. However, within the race the song was often used to express internal colour prejudice; the three types contrasted would be black, brown and yellow. For black/white antipathy we must look long, among the commercial discs. Working in the field, Paul Oliver recorded an extraordinary *Kill That Nigger Dead* (A11) from Butch Cage and Willie Thomas:

> Black nigger baby, black feet and shiny eyes,
> Black all over to the bone and india-rubber thighs;
> > Turn that nigger round and knock 'im in the head,
> > 'Cause white folks say 'We're gonna kill that nigger dead.'

A black man might have composed the song in a spirit of bitter summing-up, and it was collected from Alabamian blacks around 1915, but it was also recorded by a white stringband in the late 'twenties, so its race-of-origin is in doubt. As a rabble-rouser among nigger-haters it could doubtless have done an effective job.

So too, perhaps, could some of the early recordings of racist-sounding material, of which – since I have been unable to hear them – I can only offer the reader the titles; Fisher Hendley's *Nigger, Will You Work?* of 1925, Herschel Brown's *Talking Nigger Blues* (1928), Uncle Dave Macon's *Run, Nigger, Run*, probably the most famous version of this old slavery-days coon-hunt hymn, which was widely sung by blacks too. Uncle Tom Collins – despite his name, a white man from Georgia – sang *Every Race Has A Flag But The Coons*, a popular song of 1900. (*All Coons Look Alike To Me* had appeared four years earlier; and that one was written by a *black*.) 1900 also saw *Just Because She Made Dem Goo-Goo Eyes*, which may have contributed to, or come from the same root as, Gus Cannon's *Can You Blame The Colored Man*, which described Booker T. Washington's dinner at the White House with Theodore Roosevelt, in 1901. Both Washington and the President were bitterly criticised by southerners for this disgraceful breach of racial propriety, and Cannon's depiction scarcely dignifies the episode . . .

> Now could you blame the colored man for makin' dem
> > goo-goo eyes?
> And when he sat down at the President's table he began to
> > smile;
> > Eatin' lamb, ham, chicken roast,
> > Chicken, turkey, bread or toast,
> Now could you blame the colored man for makin' dem
> > goo-goo eyes?

'Low pitch' medicine-show at Huntingdon, Tenn., 1935, with blacked-up black artist.

Newman Ivey White, at the close of his remarks on 'Race-Consciousness', wrote 'if he (i.e. the Negro singer) is consistent in contrasting raccoon, 'possum, and rabbit, the yaller gal and the black gal, the ladybug and the bedbug, sometimes in the very same song in which he contrasts Negro and white man and always in the same manner, I am led to suppose that the real importance of the circumstance is not self-pity, but a fondness for the rhetorical device of antithesis, let the sentiments be what they may. Of course the Negro laborer is sometimes . . . dissatisfied with his lot. But the real significance of his songs expressing race-consciousness is the fact that they show so little of this mood.' And the real significance of *that* fact, surely, is that it masked from White, and from many commentators upon black song, the true feelings of the black population – feelings that were sublimated in animal antitheses because there was no other safe way of expressing them. Despite his obvious humanity and perceptiveness, White failed to see beyond the 'happy darky' superstructure; he fell a victim, as had those earlier slave-owners who thought 'coon songs' authentic black music, to minstrel stereotypes. 'To the folk Negro the music, and not the words, is the important matter'; perhaps he would have seen the fallacy of this belief if he had listened more closely to the blues, but unfortunately he thought that 'the value of the blues as an expression of the folk-Negro's mind is somewhat impaired by the fact that the folk blues and the factory product are to-day almost inextricably mixed.' (Which was half true, but much less harmful than he imagined.) He did see that the blues 'illustrate the singer's desire to comment upon himself', but he supposed that they 'do not speak for the groups, but only for the singer. They sometimes show self-pity, but it is most distinctly personal and without racial tinge. The white man, and the Negro *as* Negro, have no place in them.' Of course, the mass of blues give him superficial support; well-known lines like 'I'm blue, black and evil, and I did not make myself', or 'I can hear my black name ringing', are exceptions rather than representatives. Yet racial consciousness underlies even the most explicitly personal blues; the peculiar savour of the music rises from something more than individual emotion about love affairs and hunger and joblessness and solitude. In the commercial recordings, blues are often a dragon, and the blues singer who goes out to meet it a St George on the black community's payroll; the race record is a three-minute film of the battle. If the dragon were only a personal demon, like Robert Johnson's 'hell hound on my trail', or the voodooesque 'Mr Blues' who comes 'walking through the wood' in Little Brother Montgomery's song, then the singer might, in his five or six verses, begin to exorcise it; but too often St George is forced back against the wall, or the fight ends in an uneasy draw. For the dragon represents many public interests, particularly segregation. 'When I sing the blues,' says John Lee Hooker, '. . . it's not . . . that I had the hardships that a lot of people had throughout the South and other cities throughout the country, but I do know what they went through . . . it's not only what happened to you – it's what happened to your fore-parents and other people. And that's what makes the blues.' One of Charley Patton's songs was *Mean Black Moan*; the three words make a concise definition of the blues, but the central one, in *every* sense, is 'black'.

Out West

'The blues come to Texas,' sang Blind Lemon Jefferson, 'lopin' like a mule'. This is poetry, not history; cowboy song, however, did lope out of Texas, and white country music has worn a saddle ever since. The uniform of the country artist is the cowboy's – albeit a grotesque, besequined version; the music that blares out of Opry and a hundred other stations is called country-&-western, and the Western Swing of Texas and Oklahoma is one of its strongest strains. The Old West myth appeals more than any other because it embodies so many traditional American virtues: self-reliance, rugged individuality, respect for women, love for mother: in short, the pioneer spirit. (How astute the decision to locate the US space programme in Houston!) Cowboy song has no black affiliations, though there have been black cowboys, and Leadbelly – an exception to every generalisation about race music – used to sing *Out On The Western Plains* (26.4) and other such. Indeed, there is not much of real western music in modern C & W, for confusion rose very early between genuine material, by men like Jules Allen and Carl T. Sprague (see A49), and nostalgic recreations like Jimmie Rodgers' *Yodeling Cowboy* (37.5).

Black and white traditions have not often drawn together in Texas, but Louisiana, lying between it and Mississippi, has been something of a melting-pot for styles from east and west. Southern Louisiana enjoys a strong tradition of cajun music, which has created a vivacious substyle among the local blacks: 'zydeco'. The distinguishing characteristics of cajun and zydeco are the instrumentation – accordion and fiddle are most favoured – and the repertoire of old French dance tunes, now much augmented by

Carl T. Sprague

SPRAGUE, CARL T.—Tenor with Guitar

Bad Companions	19747	If Your Saddle Is Good
Boston Burglar	20534	Last Great Round Up
Cowboy	21402	Last Longhorn
Cowboy Love Song	20067	Mormon Cowboy
Cowboy's Dream	20122	Oh Bury Me Not on Prairie
Cowboy's Medi-		Rounded Up in Glory
tation	V-40197	Two Soldiers
Cowman's Prayer	21402	Utah Carroll
Following Cow Trail	20067	Wayward Daughter
Gambler	20534	When the Work's
Here's to the Texas		All Done
Ranger	V-40066	

HACKBERRY RAMBLERS

B-2002	Green Valley Waltz Bring It Down to the Jailhouse, Honey
B-2003	Jolie Blonde Mermentan Stomp
B-2035	Oh Josephine, My Josephine—FT La Breakdown a Pete—FT
B-2056	Une Pias ici et une Pias la Bas One Step de L'Amour
B-2059	Dans le Grand Bois French Two-Step
B-2065	Jolie Fille—Waltz (Pretty Girl) La Valse du Vieux Temp (Old-Time Waltz)

Western Swing, blues, country ballads and pop. Cajun music was very much a localised tradition in the 'twenties and before, but the success of the Riverside Ramblers, who reputedly sold a million copies of the wailing, sentimental *Wondering* in the late 'thirties, helped to focus interest from the larger world; and similar atten-

tion came in the 'fifties when a fiddler named Harry Choates put out a raw 'French Western Swing', which popularised the steel guitar among cajuns and showed that the old one-steps, two-steps and waltzes were commercially viable. Black music was always quite well received along the bayous, and blues standards like *Trouble In Mind*, sung in either English or French, or both, established themselves in everyone's repertoire. (The Hackberry – i.e. Riverside – Ramblers have recorded a bilingual *Trouble In Mind*, as *Fais Pas Ca*; 21.1.) The long-drawn moaning of the accordion may be adapted surprisingly well to blues, and artists like Iry Le June – one of the best loved of all cajun figures – could put over *Grand Bosco* and similar slow blues with powerful impact. Moreover, the constricted, high-pitched singing style of the cajun has great blues 'feel', and can be very reminiscent of Blind Lemon. Indeed, Jefferson's *Black Snake Moan* has been recorded by Clifton Chenier (13.3), a popular accordionist whose tough singing and amplified playing are well known in the bars of Louisiana and East Texas. Chenier's repertoire includes the country ballad *I Can't Stop Loving You* (13.2), Louis Jordan's *Let The Good Times Roll* (as *Bon Ton Roulet*, 13.2) and, of course, the theme which gave his music its name, *Zydeco Et Pas Sale* (13.1, A6) – 'no salt in your snap-beans!' Such pieces, interspersed with dance-tunes catering for waltzers, one- and two-steppers, stompers and breakdowners, make up a wide and exciting programme, which, nowadays, has probably more acceptance within the race – in this part of the world – than any other black tradition anywhere else. Zydeco is not the striking instance of interaction it may seem to be, for its exponents are usually doing no more than reproducing an inherited collection of tunes and songs; but it is an outstanding example of a common stock like that which I have described as existing in the 'pre-blues' era, towards the end of the nineteenth and in the early years of the twentieth century, for the evening's entertainment which a zydeco group will give you is not easily distinguishable, in selection or treatment, from that of a cajun band.

Those are the sounds of southern Louisiana; further north French music has less hold. Shreveport, for one, was a strong blues town in the 'forties and 'fifties, with many black artists playing the cafés and pavement of Texas Avenue. John Lomax visited the place in October 1940 to make some recordings for the Library of Congress, and he wrote in his field notes of three musicians he found: 'Oscar (Buddy) Woods, Joe Harris, Kid

West are all professional Negro guitarists and singers of Texas Avenue . . . The songs I have recorded are those they use to cajole nickels from the pockets of listeners. One night I sat an hour where the group was playing in a restaurant where drinks were served. I was the only person who dropped a contribution in the can. I doubt if the proprietor paid them anything.'

Harris and West played Lomax a selection of blues and rags, also *Nobody's Business If I Do*, *Bully Of The Town* and *Old Hen Cackle*, West's mandolin complementing Harris' guitar. Woods sang *Boll Weevil* and some blues, as well as his own composition *Don't Sell It – Don't Give It Away*, which he had twice recorded a few years earlier. Lomax may not have known that in Oscar Woods he had traced a musician of considerable interest, both as bluesman – he inspired Babe Kyro Lemon Turner, 'The Black Ace', to follow his steel guitar style, so that we can today hear his music in another guise than on his scarce recordings – and as that rare phenomenon, the black artist who worked with whites. For Woods not only played on a white man's records, but even sang with him – a circumstance without parallel, I think, in country music discography. This would not be more than a scholar's footnote, were it not that the affair was quite informative about the appeal of the blues to white southerners.

The white man was Jimmie Davis, who has been enshrined in the relevant history books as the composer-singer of *You Are My Sunshine*, which – it is said – propelled him firmly to the State Capitol in Baton Rouge, where he served as Governor in 1944–48 and 1960–64. ('How,' his opponents asked, 'can you fight a song?') He had worked his way through school, partly by teaching yodelling, and during the late 'twenties and 'thirties built a large following with numerous records and personal appearances. While touring he safeguarded his voice with goat's milk. The middle and late 'thirties saw him a stalwart of the Decca list, both as singer of sentimental and novelty songs and as song writer for Buddy Jones and others. His earlier work has been dismissed by Shelton as Rodgers-imitation, but this is not the half of it. Though he was fond of pieces in the blue yodel vein, he made a distinct, if less influential, contribution to white blues, by exploring the world of sexual symbolism with a wit and metaphorical command that were typically black. Songs like *She's A Hum Dum Dinger From Dingersville*, *Sewing Machine Blues*, *Bear Cat Mama From Horner's Corners*, *Yo Yo Mama* and *Triflin' Mama Blues* must have been dubious recommendations for public office, and it is said that

Davis, while campaigning, had frequently to answer accusations of mixing with blacks. Some of the songs do rather support the suggestion.

> I got the world in a jug, stopper in my hand, (*twice*)
> And I got a triflin' mama, tom-cattin' with another man.

> You ain't foolin' me, pretty mama, 'cause I got your low-
> down; (*twice*)
> You've got another sidetrack, and you sure Lord are
> switchin' around.

> Now you triflin' women sure do make me tired; (*twice*)
> Got a handful o' gimme, mouthful o' much obliged.

> Went home this mornin', as the clock was strikin' five;
> (*twice*)
> And I found another daddy gettin' honey from my
> beehive.

It could easily have been a black man's song; indeed, the opening line and the third stanza are very common in blues. It seems certain that Davis had been listening either to black records or to black musicians in his home area – Shreveport – or both. The railroad image in the second verse may have come from Rodgers' *Let Me Be Your Sidetrack* (37.2) of two years earlier, or from tradition; Leadbelly used it about this time in his *See See Rider* (26.2). (Unissued takes of Rodgers' *Sidetrack*, incidentally, featured a black accompanist, the Mississippi guitarist Clifford Gibson, but on the take used for release only Rodgers' guitar can be heard. Five days later Jimmie recorded with the all-black Louisville Jug Band – a selection which *was* issued, *My Good Gal's Gone Blues* (37.2).) Though the yodel which follows each stanza puts us in familiar territory, Davis differed from Jimmie Rodgers in his explicitness; the more famous artist applied a paler shade of blue, and would not often have sung, as Davis did in *Sewing Machine Blues*,

> It ain't your fancy walk, gal, it ain't your vampin' ways;
> It's the way you do, just before the break of day.

This blues gained considerably from the full steel guitar accom-

Photograph: Jimmie Davis.

paniment of Woods, who was present throughout this Dallas session of February 1932 but may not have played on all Davis' pieces. (The report that he also accompanied Jimmie Rodgers' *Down The Old Road To Home* (37.2), made at the same location a few days earlier, is not confirmed by the issued record.) *Sewing Machine Blues* comes from a notable group of titles; the others made on that day were *Red Nightgown Blues*, *Davis's Salty Dog* and *Saturday Night Stroll*, on the last of which the two men sang in duet. *High Behind Blues*, from the previous day, is an intriguing phrase; Mississippi bluesman Jack Kelly used it to name a blues a few years later, and one wonders if he derived from Davis or invented for himself such verses as

> She turned around and she began to grin;
> 'I ain't had none of this, Lord, in God knows when!'

On the same day as he played with Davis, Oscar Woods joined

a singer/guitarist called Ed Chafer, or Schaffer, to make a couple
of blues, one the Texas classic *Flying Crow*. They had recorded
together before, in 1930, naming themselves the 'Shreveport Home
Wreckers' – which fits neatly with a Davis line in *Pea Pickin' Papa*,
'I'm an old home-wrecker from down in Texas . . .'

It seems certain that Woods was one of the black musicians
closest to Davis, and perhaps their association was extended to
travelling shows; both had found their way to Memphis in May
1930 when the Victor team was there. (So had David McCarn, a
North Carolinian who had worked in textile mills and sang dis-
illusioned compositions like *Cotton Mill Colic* and *Serves 'Em
Fine*. He was despairing of a future in music, too, but a black
artist whom he met in Memphis advised him to try the recording
men at the Auditorium. It was a moderately successful move, and
one would like to know who the acute acquaintance was; one of
the Memphis Jug Band, perhaps, or Georgia-born Kokomo
Arnold, who made his recording debut two days earlier.) Unfortunately, mist hangs over the past of Davis, Woods, Schaffer and
the rest, and a chapter of potentially immense interest lies beyond
our sight range. Most of Jimmie Davis' early, bluer discs are rare,
which suggests that his material was a little too outrageous for the
market, but *Bear Cat Mama* and *Hum Dum Dinger* were re-

released as a cheap Bluebird coupling and stayed in catalogue well into the war years, spurring 'cover' versions by Gene Autry and others.

A noteworthy feature of his work was the retention of black and brown gals in the lyrics of his black-derived songs. Jimmie Rodgers was usually careful to give no racial hints, but Davis – who was not best known for his liberal views when in office – could cheerfully declare

> Gonna telephone to Heaven, to send me an angel down;
> If you haven't got an angel, Saint Peter, send me a
>   high-steppin' brown.

Similarly Dick Justice's *Brown Skin Blues* (A9), a melee of stock phrases and verses from Blind Lemon's *Black Horse Blues* (25.1, 3) and *Stocking Feet Blues*, expresses a wish to 'laugh . . . and talk with that long-haired brown o' mine'; while Goebel Reeves' catalogue of sexual experiences, *I Learned About Women From Her*, tells how he stole 'the wife of a nigger', who 'stabbed me one night when I wished she was white'. This sort of thing can be quite unremarkable, for many whites, in performing 'nigger blues', are going through an accepted act, and have no reason to bleach the female characters who occur in such songs; on the other hand, Reeves' composition, and no doubt others, suggests that the sociologist might unearth useful information in this field concerning the attitudes of the poor white.

He would find good things, too, in the topical and occupational compositions of the 'thirties. Decca's Buddy Jones put out *Taxicab Driver's Blues*; Ted Daffan wrote *Truck Drivers' Blues*; Fiddlin' John Carson came back to the studios and remade *Taxes On The Farmer Feeds Them All*. Now and then the black community came out in sympathy; there were Peetie Wheatstraw's *Truckin' Thru' Traffic* and *Chicago Mill Blues*, while his *Working On The Project* was only one of dozens of black comments on the New Deal. But the recording activity in northern cities which stimulated these observations was not matched by any 'urban hillbilly' development; to stock their old-time lists Bluebird and Decca and A.R.C. had to go south. Not, as once, to the southeastern states, or at least not so much; the big new sound came from Texas and Oklahoma, an amalgam of blues, jazz and the south-eastern string band tradition with the local cowboy songs. It was called Western Swing.

It is an enigma to many followers of country music. Some solve it by deciding that authentic hillbilly sounds died in the middle 'thirties for want of sustenance. How else can they face bands which throw at them, successively, *St Louis Blues*, *Love In Bloom*, *Fan It*, *Spanish Fandango* and *I Like Bananas Because They Have No Bones*? The Western Swing musicians rejoiced in an eclecticism more extreme than any other school's, and in doing so captured a wider audience than native folkmusic had ever had. To be just, we should probably call Western Swing a folk-*like* music – a precursor, in that sense, of rock-and-roll (which picked a few ideas from it too). The Western Swingers offered pops, new and venerable; jazz standards and boogies; classic blues and rural blues hits; instrumental rags and waltzes; music-hall and novelty songs; Mexican dance tunes and cowboys' songs of the range. Among the prominent orchestras were Bob Wills' Texas Playboys, famous for their leader's cigar, steel guitarist Leon ('take it away, Leon!') McAuliffe, and their radio show over KVOO, Tulsa, Okla. The Playboys' popularity was equalled in Texas by Milton Brown's Musical Brownies, whose fame grew apace from about 1934. The Brownies were perhaps a little less concerned with traditional country tunes, and slightly more with black material, than Wills' outfit; their records included versions of *Joe Turner Blues*, *Sitting On Top Of The World*, *You're Bound To Look Like A Monkey*, *Somebody's Been Using That Thing*, *Mama Don't Allow It* and so forth. Their *Louise Louise Blues* followed a few months after the original by black singer Johnny Temple, a solitary example of the flourishing 'cover' industry; many of the mid-'thirties blues successes were quickly made available in white form, often under the auspices of the same company. Kokomo Arnold's *Milk Cow Blues* (02.1) reappeared in Decca's hillbilly series, performed by Bob Wills' brother Johnny Lee; it also contributed distinctive touches to Bob's own *Brain Cloudy Blues*, among others. Likewise, *Kansas City Blues* was reworked by Leon's Lone Star Cowboys. And the longest-selling Western Swing hit of all was Wills' *Steel Guitar Rag* backed with *Swing Blues No. 1* (both A23), which could hardly have owed more to black music. The instrumental side was a modernised treatment of Sylvester Weaver's 1923 *Guitar Rag* (A43); *Swing Blues No. 1* took at least one of its verses from a hiding place ten years deep: Blind Lemon's *Long Lonesome Blues* (25.5). There was nothing accidental in this. 'Sleepy' Johnson, who played guitar and banjo with the Playboys, remembers how the Fort Worth musicians

15975 New Ulm—Polka
15975 No One Knows

CLARENCE WILLIAMS
and His Orchestra

2541 Beer Garden Blues
2541 Breeze

COOTIE WILLIAMS
and His RUG CUTTERS

5618 Black Butterfly
5618 Blues A Poppin'
5690 Dry Long So
3960 Echoes of Harlem
5690 Give It Up
3960 Lost in Meditation

BOB WILLS
and His Texas Playboys
(Hot String Band with Singing)

04275 Alexander's Ragtime Band
03578 Back Home Again in Indiana
03344 Basin Street Blues
04999 Beaumont Rag
05905 Big Beaver
03139 Black & Blue Rag
04132 Black Rider
05523 Blue Bonnet Rag
05333 Blue Prelude
03230 Blue River
03614 Bluin' the Blues
05694 Bob Wills' Special
03492 Bring It On Down to My House
05079 Carolina in the Morning
04755 Convict and the Rose
05282 Don't Let the Deal Down
05161 Dreamy Eyes Waltz
05282 Drunkard Blues
04184 Empty Bed Blues
04132 Everybody Does It in Hawaii
03361 Fan It
03076 Four or Five Times
04275 Gambling Polka Dot Blues
03451 Get Along Home Cindy
03096 Get With It
03086 Good Old Oklahoma
03206 I Ain't Got Nobody
03173 I Can't Be Satisfied
03264 I Can't Give You Anything But Love
05637 I Don't Lov' A Nobody
04439 I Wish I Could Shimmy Like My
       Sister Kate

04566 I Wonder If You Feel the Way I Do
05228 If I Could Bring Back My Buddy
05079 Ida Red
03659 I'm a Ding Dong Daddy
       (From Dumas)
04184 Keep Knocking
04625 Little Girl, Go and Ask Your Mama
04325 Little Red Head
04839 Liza Pull Down the Shades
05637 Lone Star Rag
04387 Loveless Love
03924 Maiden's Prayer
03492 Mean Mama Blues
05523 Medley of Spanish Waltzes
03086 Mexicali Rose
04439 Moonlight and Roses
05161 My Window Faces the South
03264 Never No More Blues
03924 Never No More Hard Times Blues
05694 New San Antonio Rose
03693 New St. Louis Blues, The
03537 No Matter How She Done It
05597 No Wonder
04515 Oh, Lady Be Good
04515 Oh, You Beautiful Doll
03295 Oklahoma Rag
03295 Old Fashioned Love
03693 Oozlin' Daddy Blues
03096 Osage Stomp
05401 Pray for the Lights to Go Out
05228 Prosperity Special
03344 Red Hot Gal of Mine
03451 Right or Wrong
03659 Rosetta
04755 San Antonio Rose
03424 She's Killing Me
04934 Silver Bells
03139 Sittin' on Top of the World
05333 Sophisticated Hula
03230 Spanish Two Step
03394 Steel Guitar Rag
03997 Steel Guitar Stomp
03076 St. Louis Blues
03361 Sugar Blues
03997 Sunbonnet Sue
03394 Swing Blues No. 1
03578 Swing Blues No. 2
05753 That Brownskin Gal
04566 That's What I Like 'Bout the South
05905 There's Going to Be a Party
05753 Time Changes Everything
03537 Too Busy!
03343 Trouble in Mind
04325 Tulsa Stomp
05401 Twinkle Twinkle Little Star
04999 Waltz You Saved for Me, The
03173 Wang Wang Blues
04387 Way Down Upon the Swanee River
03343 Weary of the Same Ol' Stuff
03424 What's the Matter with the Mill?
03614 White Heat
04625 Whoa Babe
03206 Who Walks in When I Walk Out
04934 Yearning
05597 You Don't Love Me
04839 You're Okay

BARRY WOOD
and His Music

5185 After I Say I'm Sorry
5185 Ciribiribin
5159 Leanin' on the Ole Top Rail
5159 South of the Border

used to gather round the phonograph in a local store and learn all the latest race hits. Lead singer Tommy Duncan had a mellow, sun-warmed voice, like a hillbilly Bing Crosby; and sure enough Bing 'covered' the Wills-Duncan *San Antonio Rose* and far outsold their version.

In its line-up the Western Swing Band was just a string band. Two fiddles, at least two guitars (one steel), bass, tenor banjo – not the 5-string instrument – with sometimes a piano, but no drums for the first few years. Brass and reeds were optional, but the successful groups normally employed them. Lead voice, after the singer, was either fiddle or steel guitar; in this respect there were some similarities with contemporary Chicago blues. Casey Bill Weldon ('The Hawaiian Guitar Wizard') and Kokomo Arnold were noted steel-men; the former was for a time member of a group called 'The Brown Bombers Of Swing'. This may have been one of those combos that followed Western Swing tactics and indulged in broad repertoires of jazz, blues, hillbilly song and religious material – like the Blue Chips or Norridge Mayhams' Barbecue Boys. Weldon was also one of the Hokum Boys, with Big Bill Broonzy and others, and one remembers with pleasure his gaily bawdy *Caught Us Doing It* and *Keep Your Mind On It*. Broonzy, with Carl Martin and the harmonica-player Jazz Gillum, made some interesting discs in the same year (1935) with a somewhat Western Swing-like line-up of fiddle, harmonica, guitar, piano and string bass; the State Street Boys, as they called themselves, made one of the very few black recordings of *Midnight Special*.

The Western Swing fiddle, however, was not much copied by blacks; the instrument was little heard in urban blues, and kept its place only in down-home string and jug bands, like Jack Kelly's. The Memphis Jug Band, led by Will Shade, ceased to record after 1934, when it made a set of spirited tunes that may have owed some ideas to Western Swing; the cross-talk and encouragements which the musicians threw in remind one of Bob Wills, while Charlie Burse's lunatic scat singing was closer to Cab Calloway. Burse had another recording chance in 1939, when he and another Memphian singer, James DeBerry, led swinging bands that featured trumpet and saxophones. Burse's 'Memphis

Photographs: Bill Boyd's Cowboy Ramblers (left) and the Prairie Ramblers, two of the most popular Western Swing bands.

Mudcats' played *It Makes No Difference Now*, a country ballad written by Floyd Tillman; this was also recorded by Piano Red (backed with *Hey Good Lookin'*). (Blues pianists delved into hillbilly music quite often in the postwar years; Albert Ammons, for instance, made an amazing boogie transformation of *You Are My Sunshine!*)

As Western Swing gathered momentum there came palmy days for other country artists: Gene Autry, Roy Acuff, Wilf Carter ('Montana Slim'), Bill and Cliff Carlisle. Acuff's *Wabash Cannonball* did well, and crept, for a time, into at least one black artist's repertoire. 'I didn't know too much about many blues; we had a radio down there but they all played big band stuff and country and western music. Well, hillbilly music was popular there and so I played hillbilly music on guitar and sung, like *She'll Be Comin' Round The Mountain*, and *It Ain't Gonna Rain No More* and *Wabash Cannonball* . . . At that time I didn't have no knowledge of music. I even liked those – as I call it – hillbilly music . . . And

Photograph: Roy Acuff (with fiddle) and his Crazy Tennesseeans.

when I played out on street-corners, well, I'd be playing for white folks mostly and that was the music they seemed to like better.' (Titon: March 1969). Thus Lazy Bill Lucas, talking of his early days in Cape Girardeau, Mo., around 1936–40. When he moved to Chicago he found different audiences – 'They tell you right away, "What you think I am, a hillbilly? I ain't no hillbilly." ' – and turned to piano, accompanying local bluesmen; but he has not shut his ears to country music, and a recent LP shows him at work on *Blueberry Hill* and similar stuff (29.1).

Not long after Lucas came to Chicago, a Library of Congress team supervised by Alan Lomax and John Work journeyed to Nashville, where it found a washboard band whose members included James Kelley (mandolin), Frank Dalton (guitar), Tom Carroll (tin can) and Theobald Stokes (washboard). Kelley may just have been the Jack Kelly who led the South Memphis Jug Band back in '33; the Nashville group recorded a *Kohoma Blues*, and Jack Kelly is known to have been from Mississippi, possibly from Coahoma County. The band played *Soldiers Joy* and *Arkansas Traveler*, also *You Rascal You* (for some reason always a favourite with small bands); then the washboard player demonstrated various dance tempi: breakdown, blues and swing. One cannot say, without hearing this recondite material, whether 'swing' meant, to Theobald Stokes, Western or jazz – Bob Wills or Benny Goodman. The second alternative is not so unlikely as it may seem; one of Doctor Ross's favourite breakdowns is called *Tommy Dorsey's Boogie* (38.1). (As Ross went to some pains to explain to the author, this piece is substantially the same as Walter Horton's celebrated harmonica showcase *Easy*.) Bourgeois semi-jazz did not generally make much impression upon rural blacks, though *Blues In The Night* (Mercer-Arlen, 1941) 'convincingly suggested,' as Spaeth puts it, 'the mood and style, if not the actual form, of true Negro folk-music,' and was adopted by some black artists with appropriate affection. (Doctor Ross was one; 38.2).

It would be useless to try and find extensive deposits of Western Swing in black music of the 'forties; the hard driving jazz of Kansas City had much more to offer the race, and in any case the southern audiences were moving back to a simpler sort of country blues, 'down-home' music. Economic difficulties encouraged solo performers and two- or three-man groups, while electrification could make an orchestra out of a guitar. Texan blacks emigrated westwards to the ghettos of San Francisco and Los Angeles; men like Lightnin' Hopkins covered both the back-home and the transported market by working for Gold Star in Houston and then Aladdin and Imperial in L.A. Southwestern whites showed equal fidelity to their music when they made the great trek, as *Rolling Stone* reporter John Grissim, Jr learned when interviewing a San Francisco newscaster about those years. (The quotation has been slightly and insignificantly edited.) 'KLX's manager called all the staff announcers together and said "I know you all hate the music but one of you guys is going to have to do a Western show – I don't care who does it ." Two days later "Cactus Jack" (Cliff Johnson) started playing Western stuff off tapes (you couldn't get records because of the war shortage) and the few records we had around the station. A lot of people from Oklahoma, Texas and Arkansas kept asking him to play records by Bob Wills and his Texas Playboys. He'd never heard of him but they all insisted Wills was their little tin Jesus back there in the Southwest.' Grissim goes on to reveal that Wills' appearances in the area often outdrew those by the Dorsey, Goodman and Miller orchestras. For all that they did not touch the black musicians, who developed a jazzy blues style with moaning vocals and prominent electric guitar solos; it drew upon K.C. sounds and employed the riff, but it had native Texan roots which can be heard in, for example, the 1939 recordings of Dusky Dailey and his Band.

However, Western Swing did not dominate country music in the 'thirties and 'forties. Plenty was happening in the east.

ALLEN BROTHERS

Out East

Once again, country music bloomed in eastern Tennessee and the areas encircling it, but the stringbands of Georgia and North Carolina were not surviving the Depression years at all well. Charlie Poole died of a heart attack in 1931, and his fiddle-playing companion Posey Rorer followed in 1936. Clayton McMichen left the Skillet-Lickers to form a modernist group, Riley Puckett devoted himself entirely to solo work, and Gid Tanner went back to his chicken farm. At their last Victor session in 1932 the Original Carolina Tar Heels sang *Times Ain't Like They Used To Be*, which exactly described both the economy and the music of the south.

For one thing, there was a fashion for duets. The Allen Brothers (Austin and Lee), probably from east Tennessee, sang a series of blues accompanying themselves on banjo, guitar and kazoo; but their chief success was with the old *Salty Dog* and *Next Week Sometime* themes. Victor kept *A New Salty Dog* (A50) in catalogue for years, but partly because of the reverse side, Alton and Rabon Delmore's *Brown's Ferry Blues*.

> Hard luck papa countin' his toes; you can smell his feet
>   wherever he goes;
>   Lord, Lord, got them Brown's Ferry blues;
> Hard luck papa can't do his stuff; the trouble with him,
>   he's been too rough;
>   Lord, Lord, got them Brown's Ferry blues.

The Delmores were from Elkmont, in Limestone County, Ala., only a few miles from the state boundary with Tennessee. Adept guitarists, they were fond of the complex boogie patterns which east-coast blacks were developing; their songs often fell into the verse/refrain form of, say, Blind Boy Fuller's *I'm A Rattlesnakin' Daddy* (18.2). They sang in soft-toned, bland harmony, appropriate enough in melancholic airs like *Gonna Lay Down My Old Guitar* (which John Jackson has neatly reproduced in a half-whisper, 24.2), but monumentally unsuitable for any sort of blues but novelties, to which they largely confined themselves.

Novelty blues, indeed, were one of the most striking innovations of the 'thirties. The method was to set elaborate, witty lyrics to equally elaborate guitar parts; sometimes the yodel appeared, but often things were happening so fast that it couldn't be fitted in. Among the best exponents of the style were Bill and Cliff Carlisle and their associate Fred Kirby; typical productions were Bill's *Rattlin' Daddy*, Kirby's *I'm A Gold Diggin' Papa* and Cliff's *A Wild Cat Woman And A Tom Cat Man* (09.1). All three men owed a good deal to Jimmie Rodgers, but in their bawdy songs they progressed considerably further; Cliff's *Mouse's Ear Blues* (09.1), for instance, was about defloration, as was *Sal's Got A Meatskin* (which one of White's informants had heard among railroad gangs of Alabama blacks some twenty years before). Neither Rodgers nor even Jimmie Davis would have chosen to sing

My gal, she's got a mouse's ear,
But she's gonna lose it when I shift my gear,

or

Place the needle in that hole and do that nasty swing,

from Cliff's *That Nasty Swing* (09.2), recorded about three months

Below: Alton and Rabon Delmore, with (lower left) harmonica-player Wayne Raney. Right: Cliff Carlisle, c. 1930. Far right: Fred Kirby.

CARLISLE, SMILING BILL
—Vocal (Old Time)

02819	Bachelor's Blues
02529	Barnyard Tumble
02839	Beneath the Weeping Willow Tree
02528	Blue Eyes
02831	Copper Head Mama
02839	Cowboy Jack
02529	Don't Marry the Wrong Woman
02831	Duvall County Blues
25021	Final Farewell, The
25021	Little Dobie Shack
02528	Lost on Life's Sea
02819	Penitentiary Blues
25020	Rattle Snake Daddy
02797	String Bean Mama
02797	Sugar Cane Mama
25020	Virginia Blues

Above: Bill Carlisle, with some Vocalion titles.

before Robert Johnson's not dissimilar *Phonograph Blues*. Carlisle's instrument was the dobro, a steel resonator guitar which he played in the bottleneck fashion, drawing long, clean lines of sound behind his or his brother's vocals. Fred Kirby used one too, as in his *Deep Sea Blues*, a sturdy revamping of *Trouble In Mind*. Bill Carlisle, on the other hand, favoured the conventional guitar,

which he played with stunning speed and accuracy, often recreating on his own the complete two-guitar patterns of a Carter Family performance. His *Rattlin' Daddy*, which we have mentioned, was a popular theme; Jimmie Rodgers' cousin Jesse made one of the earliest recordings. It seems associated with, though not the same tune as, Blind Boy Fuller's composition (see above). The Carlisles sometimes worked in the Carolinas, and may have seen Fuller, but they and their ilk had no reciprocal influence upon him; his only excursions into white territory were *Cat Man Blues* (18.1), which was a version of *Our Goodman*, and *She's Funny That Way*, a tentative stab at the popular song of the same name.

The Carlisles came originally from Wakefield, Ky. Cliff had early experience of blues playing with a young relation, Lillian Truax, who sang low-down blues and could also play guitar. He toured with shows as a yodeller and Hawaiian guitarist, and his recorded repertoire embraces every kind of country song: sentimental, western, religious and novelty. Pieces like *Ash Can Blues* and *Rooster Blues* (09.2) owed their notions to black music, but often he used an ingenuity and turn of phrase foreign to that tradition, and closer to Jimmie Rodgers. This is not to say that black song in the 'thirties was less inventive; but it aimed either for a tough, jivey language or for subdued lyricism. The two approaches are well exemplified by, respectively, Peetie Wheatstraw and Leroy

Left: Cliff Carlisle in 1957. Right: Jesse Rodgers.

Above: Cliff Carlisle (seated) with singer-yodeller-guitarist Wilbur Ball, both wearing Hawaiian leis.

Carr. Each of these artists also illustrates a link with the white singers; Wheatstraw, in *Third Street's Going Down* and others, commented upon his urban surroundings and on the post-Depression relief programmes rather as southerners described their industrial revolution (cotton-mills especially) or supported local politicians against the Washington machine (as they thought of it); Carr, on the other hand, occasionally sang melancholy ballad-like compositions, his accompanist Scrapper Blackwell filling in with dreamy mock-Hawaiian work on guitar.

Carr and Blackwell were one of the few blues duos of the 'thirties. The prevailing sound was that of the urban group; migration patterns had made the northern cities of New York, Chicago and Detroit the centres of black musical development. Unlike white singers, the blacks had no attachment to down-home country, and their songs reflect the confrontation with city life and, sometimes, with self-betterment.

> I have my books in my hand, I'm goin' 'cross to the
> Booker T.;
> I'm goin' to get Mr So-and-So to teach me my ABC.
> Washboard Sam, *Booker T. Blues*

If a musician had the country twang in his voice, it soon disappeared. William 'Jazz' Gillum, from Bessemer, Ala., sang a *Sarah Jane* which came from the same root as the white song *I Was Born Ten Thousand Years Ago* (compare also Charlie Poole's *I'm The Man That Rode The Mule 'Round The World*); that was at his second session, and he was never to go so far from the blues again.

This urbanising of the blues may be contrasted with the efforts of many eastern whites to revive old time traditions. The brothers Bill and Earl Bolick, from Hickory, N.C., did a great deal to re-popularise the ballads and broadsides of the two previous centuries, such as *The Butcher's Boy* and *Mary Of The Wild Moor*. Calling themselves the Blue Sky Boys, playing guitar and mandolin, and singing in delicate harmony, they quickly made a name in North Carolina, aided by exposure over WBT, Charlotte. This work came their way through J. W. Fincher, the local representative of the Crazy Water Crystals Co. (a patent medicine manufacturer) and an enthusiastic hirer of hillbilly musicians. He also employed Howard and Dorsey Dixon, who played steel and conventional guitar respectively, in the manner of Darby and Tarlton (whom they knew well). Like the Bolicks, they sang much religious material; *What Would You Give In Exchange For Your Soul?* was recorded in Parts 1 to 5, and *Maple On The Hill* – which Jimmie Tarlton says he wrote – stimulated several versions, as well as an *Answer To . . .* The best known *Maple On The Hill*, though, was by Mainer's Mountaineers.

J. E. Mainer was doffing and piecing-up in a Concord, N.C., cotton-mill about the same time as Blind Boy Fuller was busking

Mainer's Mountaineers – one of several line-ups. J. E. with fiddle.

in the tobacco town of Winston-Salem. A fine old-time fiddler, he drew about him a band which included many musicians who went on to considerable fame on their own. They drew from the string band tradition, recording – as Charlie Poole and the Skillet-Lickers had done – *Watermelon On The Vine, Take Me Home To The Sweet Sunny South, John Henry* and others; but they imitated the action of the Western Swingers in combining this common stock material with newer sentimental and religious compositions. The

'Crazy Mountaineers' came to the attention of bandleader Fisher Hendley, whose 'Aristocratic Pigs' were advertising sausage-meat over WBT; soon Mainer and his men were on the Crazy Water payroll. They made their recording debut in August 1935 – some two weeks after Blind Boy Fuller did – and they have been playing, though with changes in personnel, ever since. Now seen as exponents of what might be called proto-bluegrass, they are popular among folksong enthusiasts.

The band had an excellent singer, yodeller and guitarist in 'Daddy' John Love, who sounded like a cross between Jimmie Rodgers and Bill Carlisle. *Broken Hearted Blues* (33.2) took its refrain – 'my woman's done made a fool out of me' – from Jimmie's last blue yodel, but was an affecting personal creation. Similar neo-Rodgers performances were to be heard now and then from Byron Parker's Mountaineers, who made an amusing *Married Life Blues*; the quartet's reputation at present stems from the acknowledged influence of its banjoist Snuffy Jenkins upon Earl Scruggs, and thus upon the whole bluegrass movement. Scruggs' early work, which was, without exaggeration, epoch-making, was under the aegis of Bill Monroe, who also showed a fondness for crisp reworkings of Rodgers' material and similar yodelled blues. Monroe was born in 1911, a Kentuckian, and he learned much of his technique from a black fiddler and guitarist, Arnold Schultz. 'Arnold and myself,' he recalls, 'we played for a lot of square dances back in those days.' (It was Schultz' 'choke' style of guitar picking that was to influence Merle Travis.) John

Left: Jimmie Rodgers. Right: 'Daddy' John Love.

Cohen has written that 'stylistically speaking, Bill Monroe's Blue-grass was probably the finest merging of the blues and the old Anglo tradition to make a new music incorporating qualities from both', but early Monroe recordings, with his brother Charlie's guitar backing up the mandolin, show only passing references to black music, as in *Nine Pound Hammer Is Too Heavy* (A51), with its worksong phrases. (The story of bluegrass, and its black associations, must be left to the second volume of this study.)

Most of the above mentioned artists worked, travelled and recorded only in the south; black musical activity outside the northern cities, however, was remarkably poorly documented during the 'thirties. The Victor recording trip to Charlotte, N.C., in June 1936 gives a striking example of this. In nine days the company recorded the phenomenal total of 224 titles, of which less than a quarter – fifty-four – were by black musicians. Thirty-eight were of jazz or religious material; the remainder was made up of half-a-dozen by pianist 'Peg Leg' Ben Abney – one of whose songs was Fuller's *Rattlesnakin' Daddy* again – and ten by an odd singer-guitarist named Philip McCutcheon, the 'Cedar Creek Sheik', who concentrated on bawdry; 'cock for sale, buy it from the poultry man', sung in a high, almost expressionless voice, was one of the more extraordinary black offerings of the decade.

In the same town, the following year, one of the last pre-war black bands had a little session. Eddie Kelly, 'Bill' and 'Walter', playing washboard, harmonica, kazoo and guitar, made eight brisk titles, including *Come On Round To My House, Baby* and *Mama Don't Allow* (as *Shim Shaming*, A2). They may have been from Polk County, but nothing else is known of them, and they remain an anachronism in the blues milieu of 1937. So, at least, one is tempted to think, considering the flood of urban blues; but it is true that black country music may have changed more slowly. Evidence is scanty. The first generation of blues singers was dying out; Blind Lemon passed in 1930, Charley Patton in 1934, Blind Blake sometime round the mid-'thirties. Those that followed were open to sounds from the north, whether they lived there or stayed in their southern homes. So Robert Johnson drew elements of his work from Lonnie Johnson and Leroy Carr, while Mississippian neighbours of his, like Robert 'Baby Boy' Warren or Willie '61' Blackwell, experimented with words and produced cool, almost hip blues.

Robert Johnson is a good example of the black musician who seems, during the 'thirties, to be asserting the existence of the colour line and its social consequences. This was already reflected in small things; for example, family groups, particularly pairs or trios of brothers, were as common in white music as they were scarce in black. And only rarely would one find a race artist singing both secular and religious material; the black listener, if he wanted church music, did not look for it from Roosevelt Sykes or Tampa Red; he went to church. Sentimental pieces about silver-haired daddys or sweethearts of yesteryear held nothing for a black man who might never have known his father and was more concerned about the sweetheart of today. White southerners used their songs to affirm the ideals of friendship, family loyalty and old time religion – concepts outside the experience of most black people. To some extent it had always been so, but now there were more rootless, jobless and luckless blacks, the proper function of whose music was to express, and thus ease, the new hard times – not to reminisce about the old.

Yet, though the common-stock tunes and songs were being somewhat neglected, black and white traditions still met here and there. Though their records did not reflect it, many black musicians continued to play for whites and to keep their ears open to hillbilly developments. Some of country music's most influential new sounds, on the other hand, were adaptations of black models. And, underlying all the changes in musical fashion, there was a parity in the living conditions of black and white southerners; they ate the same food, spoke substantially the same language, endured the same poverty and found relief from it in similar ways. There was always an escape route in the blues for every man, since the blues could 'creep up on you and carry your mind away' whatever your colour. Not exactly the same blues; count up the troubles of the white man and then those of the black, and the second list will always be longer by one entry. But blues about 'plain old bein' lonesome . . . for a job, spendin' money, good whiskey', as Woody Guthrie put it; these blues were universal. In singing them the races almost attained a sort of union. But the barriers were not to fall; what God, in the eyes of the southern white man, had put asunder, no musical communion could join together. Which is not to say that the blues failed in anything; they had never set themselves such a task. If it is of any value that we know, from their songs, something of the lives and emotions of the blues singers, black and white, then the blues have done their business. Through them we can begin to understand what it was to be alive in that troubled world, in those troubled times. And that is a legacy we should cherish.

Bibliography

Books

ALLEN, Frederick Lewis. *Only Yesterday: An Informal History Of The Nineteen-Twenties*. Harper & Brothers, New York, 1931.

BLESH, Rudi, and JANIS, Harriet. *They All Played Ragtime*. Oak Publications, New York, 1966 (revised edition).

CHARTERS, Samuel B. *The Country Blues*. Rinehart & Co., Inc., New York, 1959. Michael Joseph Ltd., London, 1960.

CHARTERS, Samuel B. *The Bluesmen*. Oak Publications, New York, 1967.

DORSON, Richard M. *American Folklore*. Univ. of Chicago Press, Chicago, 1959.

DOYLE, Bertram Wilbur. *The Etiquette Of Race Relations In The South: A Study Of Social Control*. University of Chicago Press, Chicago, 1937.

GODRICH, John, and DIXON, Robert M. W. *Blues & Gospel Records 1902-1942*. Storyville Publications & Co., London, 1969 (revised edition).

GREENWAY, John. *American Folksongs Of Protest*. University of Pennsylvania Press, Philadelphia, 1953.

KEIL, Charles. *Urban Blues*. Univ. of Chicago Press, Chicago and London, 1966.

LAWLESS, Ray M. *Folksingers And Folksongs In America: A Handbook Of Biography, Bibliography, And Discography*. Duell, Sloan & Pearce, New York, 1960.

LAWS, Jr., G. Malcolm. *Native American Balladry: A Descriptive Study And a Bibliographical Syllabus*. (Publications of The American Folklore Society, Bibliographical and Special Series, volume 1.) The American Folklore Society, Philadelphia, 1950, revised edition, 1964.

LEADBITTER, Mike, and SLAVEN, Neil. *Blues Records: 1943-1966*. Hanover Books Ltd., London, 1968: Oak Publications, New York, 1968.

LOGAN, Rayford W. *The Negro In The United States: A Brief History*. D. Van Nostrand Co., Inc., Princeton, N.J., 1957.

MACINNES, Colin. *Sweet Saturday Night: Pop Song 1840-1920*. MacGibbon & Kee Ltd, London, 1967: Panther Arts, 1969.

MALONE, Bill C. *Country Music, U.S.A.: A Fifty-Year History*. (Publications of The American Folklore Society, Memoir Series, volume 54.) University of Texas Press for the American Folklore Society, Austin and London, 1968.

McCARTHY, Albert, *et al. Jazz On Record: A Critical Guide To The First 50 Years: 1917-1967*. Hanover Books Ltd., London, 1968: Oak Publications, New York, 1968. •

OLIVER, Paul. *Blues Fell This Morning*. Cassell & Co., Ltd, London, 1960: Collier Books, New York, 1963 (retitled *The Meaning Of The Blues*).

OLIVER, Paul. *Conversation With The Blues*. Cassell & Co., Ltd., London, 1965: Horizon: New York, 1965.

OLIVER, Paul. *Screening The Blues*. Cassell & Co., Ltd., London, 1968: Oak Publications, New York, 1970.

OLIVER, Paul. *The Story Of The Blues*. Barrie & Rockcliff, The Cresset Press, London, 1969: Chilton Books, Philadelphia, 1969.

PATTERSON, Caleb Perry. *The Negro In Tennessee, 1790-1865*. (University of Texas Bulletin No. 2205.) University of Texas Press, Austin, 1922.

RANDEL, William Peirce. *The Ku Klux Klan: A Century Of Infamy*. Hamish Hamilton Ltd., London, 1965.

RUST, Brian. *The Victor Master Book: Volume 2 (1925-1936)*. Published by the author, Hatch End, Middlesex, 1969.

SCARBOROUGH, Dorothy. *On The Trail Of Negro Folk-Songs*. Folklore Associates, Inc., Hatboro, Pa., 1963 (facsimile reprint of original 1925 edition).

SHELTON Robert, and GOLDBLATT, Burt. *The Country Music Story*. Bobbs-Merrill Co., Inc., New York, 1966.

SPAETH, Sigmund. *A History Of Popular Music In America*. Random House, Inc., New York, 1948: Phoenix House, London, 1960.

STRACHWITZ, Chris, [ed.]. *American Folk Music Occasional No. 1*. A.F.M.O., Berkeley, Calif., 1964.

WHITE, Newman I. *American Negro Folk-Songs*. Folklore Associates, Inc. Hatboro, Pa., 1965 (facsimile reprint of original 1928 edition).

Articles

BOGGS, Dock. 'I Always Loved The Lonesome Songs'. *Sing Out !* 14:3 (July 1964) 32–39.

CARTER, June. 'I Remember The Carter Family'. *Sing Out !* 17:3 (June/July 1967) 6–11.

COHEN, John. 'The Folk Music Interchange: Negro And White'. *Sing Out !* 14:6 (December 1964/January 1965) 42–49.

COHEN, John. 'Country Music Outside Nashville'. *Sing Out !* 16:1 (February/March 1966) 40–42.

COHEN, John. 'Roscoe Holcomb: First Person'. *Sing Out !* 16:2 (April/May 1966) 3–7.

COHEN, Norm. 'Tapescript: Interview with Welby Toomey (T7–197)'. *JEMF Quarterly* 5:2 (Summer 1969) 63–65.

COHEN, Norm. and Anne. 'The Legendary Jimmie Tarleton'. *Sing Out !* 16:4 (September 1966) 16–19.

GREEN, Archie. 'The Carter Family's "Coal Miner's Blues" '. *Southern Folklore Quarterly* XXV:4 (December 1961) 226–237.

GREEN, Archie. 'Hillbilly Music: Source And Symbol'. *Journal Of American Folklore* 78:309 (July-September 1965) 204–228.

GREEN, Archie. 'Dorsey Dixon: Minstrel Of The Mills'. *Sing Out !* 16:3 (July 1966) 10–13.

GREENWAY, John. 'Jimmie Rodgers – A Folksong Catalyst'. *Journal Of American Folklore* 70:277 (July-September 1957) 231–234.

GRISSIM, Jr., John. 'California White Man's Shit Kickin' Blues'. *Rolling Stone* 36 (June 28, 1969) 13–14, 17–19, 22, 24–28.

GROOM, Bob. 'The Legacy Of Blind Lemon'. *Blues World* 18 (January 1968) 14–16; 20 (July 1968) 33–37; 21 (October 1968) 30–32; 23 (April 1969) 5–7; 24 (July 1969) 9–10; 25 (October 1969) 9–10. (Continuing.)

HICKERSON, Joseph. 'Alan Lomax's "Southern Journey": A Review-Essay'. *Ethnomusicology* 9:3 (September 1965) 313–322.

KENT, Don. 'On The Trail Of Luke Jordan'. *Blues Unlimited* 66 (Oct. 1969) 4–6.

LOMAX, Alan. 'Folk Song Style'. *American Anthropologist* 61:6 (December 1959) 927–954.

MAINER, J. E. 'J. E. Mainer Of Concord, North Carolina'. *Sing Out !* 18:1 (March/April 1968) 22–27.

ODUM, Howard W. 'Folk-Song And Folk-Poetry As Found In The Secular Songs Of The Southern Negroes'. *Journal Of American Folk-Lore* 24:93 (July-September 1911) 255–294; 94 (October-December 1911) 351–396.

PANKAKE, John. 'Sam And Kirk McGee From Sunny Tennessee'. *Sing Out !* 14:5 (November 1964) 46–50.

PERROW, E. C. 'Songs And Rhymes From The South'. *Journal Of American Folk-Lore* 25:96 (April-June 1912) 137–155; 26:100 (April-June 1913) 123–173; 28:108 (April-June 1915) 129–190.

RUSSELL, Tony. 'The Kansas City Dog Walkers'. *Jazz Monthly* 168 (February 1969) 8–10.

RUSSELL, Tony. 'Key To The Bushes: Johnson Boys'. *Blues Unlimited* 67 (November 1969) 19.

SMITH, Hobart. 'I Just Got The Music In My Head'. *Sing Out !* 14:6 (January 1965) 8–15.

SPOTTSWOOD, Richard, and JASON, David A. 'Discoveries Concerning Recorded Ragtime'. *Jazz Journal* 21:2 (February 1968) 7.

TITON, Jeff. 'Calling All Cows: Lazy Bill Lucas'. *Blues Unlimited* 60 (March 1969) 10–11; 61 (April 1969) 9–10; 62 (May 1969) 11–12; 63 (June 1969) 9–10.

WELDING, Pete. 'Interview With Carl Martin'. *78 Quarterly* 1:2 (1968) 27–31.

Discography

NOTE a) American issues are given in roman type, English and Continental issues in italic;

b) after each artist's (group's) main entries are listed the code numbers of anthologies which contain material by him (it);

c) some records are listed to which there is no reference in the text; they do, however, contain relevant material.

Part 1. Records by Individual Artists and Groups

ANDERSON, Pink	01.1	Riverside RLP148 (reverse by Blind Gary Davis)
	.2	Prestige/Bluesville BVLP1038
	.3	Prestige/Bluesville BVLP1051
	.4	Prestige/Bluesville BVLP1071 and A38
ARNOLD, Kokomo	02.1	Blues Classics BC-4 (reverse by Peetie Wheatstraw)
	.2	*Saydisc/Matchbox SDR163* and A38
ASHLEY, Clarence	03.1	Folkways FA2355
	.2	Folkways FA2359 and A12, A14, A16
BLAKE, Blind	04.1	*Riverside RLP8802*
	.2	Biograph BLP12003 and A19, A32, A34, A56
BOGGS, Dock	05.1	Folkways FA2351
	.2	Folkways FH5458
	.3	Folkways FA2392 and A9, A12, A16
CAGE, Butch, and THOMAS, Willie	06.1	Folk-Lyric FL111 (with others) and A11
CAMPBELL, Blind James	07.1	Arhoolie F1015
CANNON, Gus	08.1	*RCA RCX202* (EP)
	.2	Stax 702 and A13, A16, A24, A28, A30, A31, A32, A52, A55
CARLISLE, Cliff	09.1	Old Timey X-103
	.2	Old Timey X-104 and A22
CAROLINA TAR HEELS	10.1	Folk-Legacy FSA24 and A9, A14. A22, A50, A51 See also 03.1, .2
CARTER FAMILY, The	11.1	Decca DL4404, *Ace of Hearts AH58*
	.2	Decca DL4557, *Ace of Hearts AH112*
	.3	Camden 586
	.4	Victor LPM-2772 and A14, A15, A16, A51
CHATMAN (Carter), Bo	12.1	Yazoo L-1014 and A7, A19, A35, A54

NOTE Chatman was also a member of the Mississippi Sheiks, some of whose records may be found on the following anthologies: A35, A37, A54. See also A20 (Mississippi Mud Steppers).

CHENIER, Clifton	13.1	Arhoolie F1024
	.2	Arhoolie F1031
	.3	Arhoolie F1038 and A1, A6

CHOATES, Harry	14.1	'D' 7000 and A23
DANIELS, Julius	15.1	RCA RCX7175 (EP)
		and A16, A43, A46
DIXON, Dorsey	16.1	Testament T3301
		and A22
EAGLIN, Snooks	17.1	Folkways FA2476, Storyville 670
		119
	.2	Folk-Lyric FL107
	.3	Prestige/Bluesville BVLP1046,
		XTRA 5051
	.4	Storyville SLP140
	.5	Storyville SLP146
FULLER, Blind Boy	18.1	Philips BBL7512
	.2	Blues Classics BC-11
	.3	Saydisc/Matchbox SDR143
		and A3, A7, A38, A46
GRAYSON, G. B. and WHITTER, Henry	19.1	County 513
		and A14, A18, A20, A22, A51
GUTHRIE, Woody	20.1	Elektra EKL271/2
	.2	Folkways FA2481, Topic 12T31
	.3	Victor LPV-502, RCA RD7642
HACKBERRY RAMBLERS	21.1	Arhoolie F5003
		and A20, A21, A23
HOLCOMB, Roscoe	22.1	Folkways FA2363 (reverse by
		Wade Ward)
	.2	Folkways FA2368
		and A12
HURT, Mississippi John	23.1	Piedmont PLP13157
	.2	Piedmont PLP13161
	.3	Vanguard VRS9220, SVRL19032
	.4	Vanguard VSD79248, SVRL
		19005 and A7, A12, A14, A16,
		A19, A35
JACKSON, John	24.1	Arhoolie F1025
	.2	Arhoolie F1035
		and A6
JEFFERSON, Blind Lemon	25.1	Roots RL301
	.2	Roots RL306
	.3	Milestone MLP2004, CBS/Mile-
		stone 63738
	.4	Milestone MLP2007
	.5	Biograph BLP12000
	.6	Biograph BLP12015
		and A7, A16, A19, A33, A53
LEDBETTER, Huddie (Leadbelly)	26.1	Elektra EKL301/2
	.2	XTRA 1017
	.3	Biograph BLP12013
	.4	Storyville Special 616 003
	.5	Folkways FA2941
	.6	Folkways FA2942
		and A1, A7, A36
LEWIS, Furry	27.1	Folkways FS3823
	.2	Prestige/Bluesville BVLP1036
	.3	Prestige/Bluesville BVLP1037
	.4	Blue Horizon 7-63228
		and A14, A42, A52, A55
LIPSCOMB, Mance	28.1	Arhoolie F1001
	.2	Arhoolie F1023
	.3	Arhoolie F1026
	.4	Arhoolie F1033
	.5	Reprise (9-)2012, RV2006
		and A5, A11
LUCAS, Lazy Bill	29.1	Wild 12M01

McGEE, Sam (and Kirk)　　　30.1　Folkways FA2379
　　　　　　　　　　　　　　　.2　Folkways FTS31007
　　　　　　　　　　　　　　　　　(both with Arthur Smith)
　　　　　　　　　　　　　　　　　and A9
　　NOTE　The McGee brothers frequently accompanied Uncle Dave Macon,
　　　　　q.v.
McTELL, Blind Willie　　　　32.1　Yazoo L-1005
　　　　　　　　　　　　　　　.2　*Roots RL324*
　　　　　　　　　　　　　　　.3　Melodeon MLP7323, *Storyville
　　　　　　　　　　　　　　　　　670 186*
　　　　　　　　　　　　　　　.4　Biograph BLP12008
　　　　　　　　　　　　　　　.5　Prestige/Bluesville BVLP1040,
　　　　　　　　　　　　　　　　　Prestige 1040
　　　　　　　　　　　　　　　　　and A7, A43
MACON, Uncle Dave　　　　　31.1　RBF RF51
　　　　　　　　　　　　　　　.2　Decca DL4344, *Ace of Hearts
　　　　　　　　　　　　　　　　　AH135*
　　　　　　　　　　　　　　　　　and A10, A16
MAINER, J. E.　　　　　　　33.1　Old Timey X-106
　　　　　　　　　　　　　　　.2　Old Timey X-107
　　　　　　　　　　　　　　　.3　Arhoolie F5002
　　　　　　　　　　　　　　　　　and A27, A51
MEMPHIS JUG BAND　　　　　34.1　*Collectors Classics CC2*
　　　　　　　　　　　　　　　.2　*Roots RL322*
　　　　　　　　　　　　　　　　　and A2, A7, A13, A16, A19,
　　　　　　　　　　　　　　　　　　A24, A28, A29, A30, A31,
　　　　　　　　　　　　　　　　　　A32, A42
POOLE, Charlie　　　　　　　35.1　County 505
　　　　　　　　　　　　　　　.2　County 509
　　　　　　　　　　　　　　　.3　County 516
　　　　　　　　　　　　　　　　　and A8, A14, A18, A20
PUCKETT, Riley　　　　　　　36.1　*GHP LP902*
　　　　　　　　　　　　　　　　　and A8, A10, A21
　　NOTE　Puckett was also a member of Gid Tanner's Skillet-Lickers, q.v.
RODGERS, Jimmie　　　　　　37.1　Victor LPM-1232, *RCA
　　　　　　　　　　　　　　　　　　　　　　　　RD27138*
　　　　　　　　　　　　　　　.2　Victor LPM-1640, *RCA
　　　　　　　　　　　　　　　　　　　　　　　　RD27110*
　　　　　　　　　　　　　　　.3　Victor LPM-2112,
　　　　　　　　　　　　　　　　　(a) *RCA RD27203*
　　　　　　　　　　　　　　　　　(b) *RCA RCX1058* (EP)
　　　　　　　　　　　　　　　.4　Victor LPM-2213, *RCA
　　　　　　　　　　　　　　　　　　　　　　　　RD27241*
　　　　　　　　　　　　　　　.5　Victor LPM-2531, *RCA RD7505*
　　　　　　　　　　　　　　　.6　Victor LPM-2634, *RCA RD7562*
　　　　　　　　　　　　　　　.7　Victor LPM-2865, *RCA RD7643*
　　NOTE　The 16 tracks on Victor LPM-2112 (.3) were released in England
　　　　　as a 12-track LP (.3a) and a 4-track EP (.3b).
ROSS, Doctor Isaiah　　　　38.1　*Blue Horizon LP1*
　　　　　　　　　　　　　　　.2　Testament T2206
SMITH, Hobart　　　　　　　39.1　Folk-Legacy FSA17, *Topic
　　　　　　　　　　　　　　　　　　　　　　　　12T187*
　　　　　　　　　　　　　　　　　and A12, A27, A47
STOKES, Frank　　　　　　　40.1　*Roots RL308*
　　　　　　　　　　　　　　　　　and A3, A30, A42, A52, A55, A57
STONEMAN, Ernest　　　　　41.1　Historical HLP8804
　　　　　　　　　　　　　　　.2　Folkways FA2315
　　　　　　　　　　　　　　　　　and A16, A18
TANNER, Gid and his Skillet-Lickers 42.1　County 506 and A8, A20, A50
TARLTON, Jimmie　　　　　43.1　Testament T3302
　　NOTE　Tarlton's earlier (1927–32) recordings, most of which were duets
　　　　　with Tom Darby, remain largely unreissued, but a few are on the
　　　　　following anthologies: A8, A21, A22.

TERRY, Sonny   44.1   Folkways FA2035, *Topic 12T30*
                                       .2   Folkways FA2327, *Topic 12T29*
                                             (with Brownie McGhee)
                                       .3   Riverside 12-644
                                             and A41
          NOTE   Terry sometimes accompanied Blind Boy Fuller, q.v.
THOMAS, Henry   45.1   Origin OJL3
                                             and A15, A16, A33, A36, A45,
                                             A53, A57

THOMAS, Willie: *see* Butch Cage
WARD, Fields   46.1   Historical BC-2433-1
                                       .2   Biograph RC6002
                                       .3   Biograph RC6003
WHITTER, Henry: see G. B. Grayson

Part 2. Anthologies

A1   Arhoolie F1009: 'Zydeco'
A2   Blues Classics BC-2: 'Jug, Jook, And Washboard Bands'
A3   BC-6: 'Country Blues Classics – Vol. 2'
A4   Candid CJM8026: 'A Treasury Of Field Recordings – Vol. 1' (*77 LA-12-2*)
A5   CJM8027: 'A Treasury Of Field Recordings – Vol. 2' (*77 LA-12-3*)
A6   *CBS 63912*: 'American Folk Blues Festival '69'
A7   *CBS 66218*: 'The Story Of The Blues'
A8   Columbia CS9660: 'Ballads And Breakdowns Of The Golden Era'
A9   County 511: 'A Collection Of Mountain Blues'
A10   515: 'Mountain Banjo Songs & Tunes'
A11   *Decca LK4664*: 'Conversation With The Blues'
A12   Folkways FA2390: 'Friends Of Old Time Music'
A13   FA2610: 'American Skiffle Bands'
A14   FA2951: 'Anthology Of American Folk Music – Volume One: Ballads'
A15   FA2952: 'Anthology Of American Folk Music – Volume Two: Social Music'
A16   FA2953: 'Anthology Of American Folk Music – Volume Three: Songs'
A17   Historical BC-2433-2: 'Early Country Music – Vol. 2'
A18   HLP8003: 'Traditional Country Classics 1927–1929'
A19   Melodeon MLP7324: 'The Party Blues'
A20   Old Timey X-100: 'The String Bands'
A21   X-101: 'The String Bands – Vol. 2'
A22   X-102: 'Ballads & Songs'
A23   X-105: 'Western Swing'
A24   Origin OJL4: 'The Great Jug Bands'
A25   OJL14: 'Alabama Country 1927/31'
A26   Piedmont PLP13158: 'Ragtime – A Recorded Documentary 1899–1929'
A27   Prestige/International 25009: 'Bad Man Ballads'
A28   RBF RF6: 'The Jug Bands'
A29   *Riverside RLP8802*: 'Tub Jug Washboard Bands 1924–1932,
A30   *Roots RL307*: 'The Memphis Area (1927–1929)'
A31   *RL310*: 'Missouri And Tennessee (1924–1937)'
A32   *RL311*: 'Harmonicas, Washboards, Fiddles & Jugs (1926–1933)'
A33   *RL312*: 'Texas Country Music – Vol. 1 (1927–1936)'
A34   *RL313*: '"Down South" (Louisiana-Mississippi-Alabama-Florida) (1927–1941)'
A35   *RL314*: 'Mississippi Blues – Vol. 3 (1928–1942)'
A36   *RL315*: 'Texas Country Music – Vol. 2 (1927–1937)'
A37   *RL316*: 'The Country Fiddlers'
A38   *RL318*: 'The East Coast States (Georgia-Carolinas-Virginia)'
A39   *RL319*: 'Up And Down The Mississippi'
A40   *RL320*: 'The Great Harmonica Players – Vol. 1'

A41	*RL321*: 'The Great Harmonica Players – Vol. 2'
A42	*RL323*: 'Memphis Blues – Vol. 1'
A43	*RL326*: 'The East Coast States – Vol. 2'
A44	*RL327*: 'Texas Country Music – Vol. 3'
A45	*RL328*: 'Southern Sanctified Singers'
A46	*Saydisc/Matchbox SDR168*: 'Blind Boy Fuller On Down (Vol. 2)'
A47	Vanguard VRS9182: 'Traditional Music At Newport 1964 – Part 1'
	(*Fontana TFL6049*)
A48	VRS9183: 'Traditional Music At Newport 1964 – Part 2'
A49	Victor LPV-522: 'Authentic Cowboys And Their Western Songs'
	(*RCA RD7776*)
A50	LPV-552: 'Early Rural String Bands'
A51	LPV-532: 'The Railroad In Folksong' (*RCA RD7870*)
A52	Yazoo L-1002: 'Ten Years In Memphis: 1927–1937'
A53	L-1004: 'Tex-Arkana-Louisiana Country: 1927–1932'
A54	L-1007: 'Jackson Blues: 1928–1938'
A55	L-1008: 'Frank Stokes' Dream/The Memphis Blues: 1927–1931'
A56	L-1013: 'East Coast Blues: 1924–1935'
A57	L-1018: 'Going Away Blues: 1926–1935'

Index

Note: page numbers in *italic* refer to photographs.

Abney, 'Peg Leg' Ben   101
Accooe, —   16
Acuff, Roy   90, *90*
Alabama Sheiks   58
Allen Brothers (Austin & Lee)   25, *92*, 93
Allen, Jules   78
Ammons, Albert   90
Anderson, Charles   66
Anderson, Pink   16
Anthony, Eddie   33
Arlen, Harold   91
Armstrong, Louis   64
Arnold, James 'Kokomo'   30, 57, 84, 86, 88
Ashley, Clarence 'Tom'   14, 60
Autry, Gene   85, 90

Bailey, DeFord   *53*, 54–5
Ball, Wilbur   97
'Barbecue Bob' (Robert Hicks)   39–40
Baxter, Andrew   45
Baxter, Jim   45
Binkley Brothers' Clodhoppers   55
Bird, Billy   32
Blackwell, Francis 'Scrapper'   98
Blackwell, Willie '61'   101
Blind Blake   49–50, 101
Blue Chips, The   89
Blue Sky Boys, The   20, 98
Boggs, Dock   51, *52*
Bolick, Bill & Earl *see* The Blue Sky Boys
Booker, Jim   51
Bouchillon, Chris   17, *18*
Boyd, Bill   89
Bracey, Ishman   69
Broonzy, 'Big Bill'   89
Brown Bombers Of Swing, The   88–9
Brown, Herschel   75
Brown, Lew   58
Brown, Milton   58, 86
Brown, Percy   45
Brown, Richard 'Rabbit'   43
Brown, Sammy   50–1
Burnett, Chester *see* 'Howlin' Wolf'
Burse, Charlie   89–90
Butler, Sam   43

Cage, Butch   *8*, 75
Callahan Brothers (Bill & Joe)   33
Calloway, Cab   89
Campbell, Blind James   16
Cannon, Gus   46, 75
Carlisle, Bill   90, 94, *95*, 95–6, 100
Carlisle, Cliff   66–7, 90, 94, 95, *95*, 96, 97
Carolina Tar Heels, The   14, 93
Carr, Leroy   96–8, 101
Carroll, Tom   91
Carson, Fiddlin' John   23, 26, *27*, 33, 85
Carter Family, The   15, *40*, 41, 62, 96
Carter, Wilf ('Montana Slim')   90
Carver Brothers   25
Chatman Family   25, 55–8
Chatman, Bo   55–6, *57*
Chatman, Lonnie   55
Chatman, Sam   55, *57*, 58
Chenier, Clifton   80
Choates, Harry   80

Christian, Tom   67
Christy Minstrels, The   11, 16
Clay, Beauford   16
Cole, Bob   16
Coleman, Jaybird   23
Collins, Uncle Tom   75
Cox, Bill   73–4
Crosby, Bing   88

'Daddy Stovepipe' (Johnny Watson)   *34*, 35–6
Daffan, Ted   85
Dailey, Dusky   92
Dalhart, Vernon   *28*
Dalton, Frank   91
Daniels, Julius   43, 45
Darby, Tom   32, 70–1, *71*, 72, 98
Davis, Gussie L.   13, 14
Davis, Jimmie   59, 81–5, 94
DeBerry, Jimmie   89
Delmore Brothers (Alton & Rabon)   23, 93, *94*
Delta Boys, The   74
Dixon Brothers (Dorsey & Howard)   38–9, *39*, 98
Dixon, Dorsey   41, 71
Dorsey, Georgia Tom *see* 'Georgia Tom'
Dorsey, Tommy   91, 92
Dresser, Paul   13
Driftwood, Jimmie   51
Duncan, Tommy   88
Dupree, Champion Jack   73

Eaglin, Snooks   66
Elliott, G. H.   12–3
Emmett, Dan   16
Evans, Joe   32
Evans, John   32
Everidge, Charley   51

Fincher, J. W.   98
Ford, Henry   36
Foster, Garley   14, *14*
Foster, 'Baby Face' Leroy   64
Fuller, Blind Boy   93, 96, 98–9, 100, 101

Ganus, Clarence   74
Gardner, Robert   15, *15*
'Georgia Tom'   72
Gibson, Clifford   82
Gillum, William 'Jazz'   89, 98
Goodman, Benny   91, 92
Grant Brothers (Claude & Jack)   60, *61*
Guthrie, Woody   102

Hackberry Ramblers, The   79, *79*, 80
Hall, Vera   67
Hanson, William   57
Harris, Charles K.   13
Harris, Joe   80–1
Harvey, Roy   *13*
Hayes, Nap   32–3
Helms, Bill   24
Henderson, Ray   58
Hendley, Fisher   75, 100
Henry, Waymon 'Sloppy'   36
Hicks, Robert *see* 'Barbecue Bob'
Hines, Earl   64